The following pages contain the transcript of discussions which took place at a Symposium on "Death and Attitudes Toward Death," conducted by the Bell Museum of Pathology, University of Minnesota Medical School. The material has been edited by Dr. Stacey B. Day, University of Minnesota.

The individual colloquia were conducted at week intervals and each session was recorded verbatim.

Batesville Casket Company believes that the information contained in this book, is not only interesting, but of vital importance to each of us associated with the funeral industry. In dealing with death, it is our opinion that there must be a close working relationship and understanding between funeral directors, physicians and clergymen. Because of this belief and our intense concern and dedication to funeral service, we have made this book available — not as a solution to existing problems and situations, but as an implement for provoking thought.

It is our hope that this information will foster a greater understanding of death and related attitudes, and that this understanding can be applied toward better dealings with bereaved individuals.

It should be noted that the following text does not directly reflect opinions of Batesville Casket Company, Inc. It is a collection of many opinions, of numerous individuals, of varying interests and professions.

Proceedings

Death and Attitudes Toward Death

A Symposium of the
Bell Museum of Pathology,
Department of Pathology,
University of Minnesota
   Medical School

Edited by:
Stacey B. Day, M.D., Ph.D., D.Sc.
Conservator, Bell Museum of Pathology
University of Minnesota Medical School

Published by:
The Bell Museum of Pathology,
University of Minnesota Medical
School, in association with the
Batesville Casket Company, Inc.
Batesville, Indiana

Library of Congress
Card Catalog Number 72-76821

I.S.B.N.-0-912922-01-X

Editorial Board

Panel Moderator

Stacey B. Day, M.D., Ph.D., D.Sc.,
Conservator, Bell Museum of Pathology
University of Minnesota Medical School

Panel Members

Mark G. Wood, Phase D
    Medical Student
Chairman of Medical Student
    Committee,
University of Minnesota Medical School

Dr. John Brantner,
Professor of Clinical Psychology,
University of Minnesota

Dr. I. E. Fortuny,
Associate Professor and Director,
Medicine and Cancer Tutorial
    Program,
University of Minnesota Medical School

Dr. Robert Fulton,
Professor and Associate Chairman,
Department of Sociology,
University of Minnesota

Dr. Robert A. Good,
Professor and Head,
Department of Pathology,
University of Minnesota Medical School

Chaplain Neil Hering,
House Chaplain,
University of Minnesota Hospitals

Curtis A. Herron, B.A., M. Div.,
Pastor,
Zion Baptist Church,
Minneapolis, Minnesota

Panel Members

Dr. Jasper Hopkins,
Associate Professor of Philosophy,
University of Minnesota

Nurse Florence Kahn,
Pediatric Nurse Clinician,
University of Minnesota Hospitals

Dr. B. J. Kennedy,
Professor of Medicine and
    Medical Oncology,
University of Minnesota Medical School

Father D. Edward Mathie, S.J.,
Rector,
Jesuit College,
St. Paul, Minnesota

Dr. Mark Nesbit,
Associate Professor of Pediatrics,
University of Minnesota Medical School

Mulford Q. Sibley,
Professor of Political Science,
University of Minnesota

Dr. James M. Schless,
Director, Office of Postgraduate
    Medical Education,
Associate Professor, Department
    of Medicine,
University of Minnesota Medical School

Dr. Richard Simmons,
Associate Professor of Surgery
    and Microbiology,
University of Minnesota Medical School

Robert C. Slater,
Professor and Director,
Mortuary Science Division
University of Minnesota

Regent Loanne Thrane,
Board of Regents,
University of Minnesota

Dr. George Williams,
Associate Professor,
Psychiatry and Public Health,
University of Minnesota

Acknowledgements

"Death and Attitudes Toward Death" has been made available by Batesville Casket Company in the interest of all associated with funeral service and the medical profession. It is presented in the hope that the material contained will be absorbed and applied to the better understanding of the problems of death, encountered by both professions.

Acknowledgement is given to the faculty members of the University of Minnesota for their keen interest and cooperation which made the symposium possible Special thanks are extended to Mrs. Mary Helen Hanson, for undertaking the burden of additional work beyond her duties at the University.

Appreciation is also given to Nasreen Day, M.A., for editorial contribution, proofreading and manuscript research, and to Mr. Douglas Reynolds for the recording of all sessions.

Special acknowledgement is given to the Student Medical Council and the Medical Student Body, for their interest, cooperation and assistance, without which the symposium could not have been held.

Recognition is given to the Minnesota Funeral Directors Association and the National Funeral Directors Association for their support and contributions toward presentation of the program.

Table of Contents

Acknowledgements

Introduction   Page 13

Colloquium I . . . .
**Death—The Adult and
The Physician**   Page 17
Stacey B. Day
Robert Fulton
Richard Simmons
John Brantner
Mulford Q. Sibley
B. J. Kennedy
Mark G. Wood

Colloquium II . . . .
**Death—The Physician,
Patient, Hospital Personnel
and Relatives**   Page 35
Stacey B. Day
Neil Hering
Richard Simmons
John Brantner
I. E. Fortuny
Robert Slater
Robert Good
Loanne Thrane
Mark G. Wood

Colloquium III . . . .
**Death—The Child Patient
and the Physician**   Page 55
Stacey B. Day
D. Edward Mathie
George Williams
John Brantner
Mark Nesbit
Mulford Q. Sibley
Florence Kahn
Jasper Hopkins
Mark G. Wood

Death and the Black   Page 77
Stacey B. Day
Curtis A. Herron

A Closing Note   Page 93

Introduction

When I was born I was given the name Etok.
What does Etok mean?
It has no meaning!
I don't understand. Why not?
Until I die. Then the meaning and definition
  of the name Etok will be written.
How?
The meaning and how of Etok has lived.

(A cultural custom of the Esquimaux is on occasion to create a new name for a child. They say that the interpretation of the name is fulfilled upon the death of the child — when a second ceremony celebrates the name.

.... Stacey B. Day)

It has been said that ever since men began to think, the subject of death has exercised their minds. However, it is true that only in these last few years have the conditions and circumstances of dying become of increasing impor- tance and concern, not only to profes- sional health care deliverers, but to society as a whole. This wide interest is of importance and, fortunately, now far removed from the words of Edward Young, who once asked:

"Who can take Death's portrait? The tyrant never sat."

Certainly not the physician alone, for the study of human ideas of death, derives much of its perspective from human aspects of life. The aspects of the one are naturally and mutually more or less dependant on and modified by aspects of the other. So it is in this sense that others, in addition to physicians, are equally and critically concerned in issues of death and dying - and rightly so. Sociologists, Psychologists, Psychiatrists, Social and Literary Historians, Mortuary Scientists, Theologians, Philosophers, Cultural Anthropologists, as well as others, including physicians, have a vital interest in considering the problem. Involvement in questions of death raises issues far beyond scientific matters in our technological societies of today. Ethical, religious, social and humanitarian considerations all must be considered if humanity, as a whole, is to better progress and undertake possibilities for more wholesome growth in life. Suicide and euthanasia, contraception or abortion, heart transplants and high costs of such innovative surgery, pharmacologic prolongation of "life" and the reward of a "few more days to live", all present single aspects of death only to the unwise. The wise man (and how few persons are so wise) better sees that his understanding of death can only increase by multidisciplinary learning. Significant medical advances resulting from research and technology, commendable as they are, have little meaning unless vision is clearly held of other aspects of living (and dying) that are better seen through the eyes of the social scientist, clergyman and theologians, lawyers and anthropologists. Death education stems from contributions of all these men and of the disciplines they represent. And it is exciting to know that these feelings are felt by contemporary medical students and the general student body who are committed to ask of their teachers questions, and to demand not superficial or exotic reasoning, not blind adherence to outdated dogma or doctrine, but an effort to arrive at underlying reasons, as well as physiologic processes of living and of life. The present student and social body would, I suspect, find Spinoza's proposition that "the proper study for a wise man is not death, but how to live" too limiting. Though a wise man be not guided by fear of death but by a direct desire of good, we have arrived in our generation at a point in time where death, no less than life, offers a wise study to a sensitive man. To Goethe's advice, "Gedenke zu leben" (think how to live) we must add an addendum that would read, "and think how to die." In this symposium, the medical student body raised questions, important questions, for themselves as young men in training and for themselves as future physicians and doctors of all specialities. These questions are important for their patients, for their family and for society as a whole; and important for the growth process of their teachers and professional instructors.

Few medical schools, if any, offer

a truly perceptive, dimensional course of instruction on death. For to be valid, as we have argued, such a course must be tutored by men who may be philosophers, sociologists, prelates, anthropologists, historians - who may in fact be drawn from *all* faculties of the university as well as from the Medical School.

Such an integrative view, based on multidisciplinary knowledge is, we feel, the one approach to the subject best suited to the demands of our increasing technological society imposing itself about and upon our people as individuals.

Meditation on death is no unworthy pursuit. This presentation - these colloquia - are not offered in the vain hope that they have covered or solved all problems of death. But, raised by medical students seeking answers, the observations presented here entertain a hope that they will provoke that thought process by which each reader or audience member may a little more easily attain *his own self-understanding* of the subject discussed and deliver of himself an attitude towards problems of death that he may encounter in his own professional and social living.

These colloquia, as presented, were overwhelmingly supported by the faculty and student body. They present part of the ongoing Curriculum Development Program of the Bell Museum of Pathology and Department of Pathology of the University of Minnesota Medical School. It is with excitement and happiness that we recognize that such multidisciplinary approaches in medical school education can only be effected by the *real* interest of the medical student body acting through their representatives - the Medical Student Council, in cooperation with other faculties and non-medical departments of the University. This symposium, we believe, has offered great encouragement, not only to the field of death studies, but also in bringing before the medical student body the need for awareness of the wider role played by sociologists, psychologists, religious personnel, mortuary scientists, humanitarian and other representative disciplines in professional health education and in the education of society in general.

Limitations set upon our sessions made a fourth seminar, devoted to attitudes toward death of blacks, not publicly possible, but Pastor Curtis A. Herron has contributed a special concluding discussion that we hope will significantly contribute toward the growth, development and understanding of all, students and faculty alike.

Death effects blacks no less than whites - indeed how often has it been said that death is the great leveler:

"Et dans ces grands tombeaux,
      ou leurs âmes hautaines
Font encore les vaines
      ils sont mangés des vers."

Wealth, power, social standing is "eaten by worms" - the rich and the great, the poor and the unfortunate, the black and the white, the beautiful and the ugly, the strong and the weak; all titles are levelled in death:

"Think in this battered Caravanserai,
Whose portals are alternate Night and
   Day
How Sultan after Sultan with his pomp
Abode his destined hour, and went his
   way."

Men seek a unity in one human humanity. The observations of Pastor Herron, with regards to blacks, can guide us to understand, with sympathy and sensitivity, attitudes toward death in *all* our patients, black and white. This also involves their needs and the needs of their families, so that our response as physicians is truly to *all* men no matter their race, color, creed or station in life.

Stacey B. Day, M.D., Ph.D., D. Sc.
Robert A. Good, M.D., Ph.D.

Death—The Adult and The Physician

DR. JAMES SCHLESS: I would like to introduce Dr. Stacey Day, Conservator of the Bell Museum of Pathology, who will introduce us to members of the panel.

DR. STACEY DAY: Thank you Jim. In order to get the protocol under way I should say that most of the questions that we have, were given to us by the medical students. Mark Wood has brought and sorted these questions. Obviously there is a far greater number of questions than we can hope to answer in just three panel sessions. I hope you will all just relax and I will direct some of the questions to members of the panel who will respond, I hope, and perhaps be provocative in their answers.

Our primary aim was to get a mixed panel that was not made up entirely of physicians. I think we have a very distinguished panel. We have Dr. Bob Fulton who is in his own area completely in a Death Symposium. He is Associate Chairman of the Department of Sociology and Professor of Sociology in the University of Minnesota. We also have Professor Mulford Q. Sibley of the Department of Political Science, who is standing in for one who I think was a very dear friend of many of us - certainly those who knew him. Dr. John Berryman was to have been in attendance, but his story is known to you all. I don't think anybody can step into his shoes, in any way, but Mulford Sibley was recommended as a peer for the third panel by John Berryman, and we are happy to welcome him now. We have with us John Brantner, Professor of Clinical Psychology, who will be a companion with us through all three panels.

From our medical school faculty we shall have in the first session a transplant surgeon. Dr. Dick Simmons is Associate Professor of Surgery and Microbiology. Dr. B. J. Kennedy, Professor of Medicine, will represent the Department of Medicine and Medical Oncology. Mark Wood will represent the Student Medical Council and the student body.

MARK WOOD: I would like to start the first question with a preface phrased from an editorial in Science (19 June 1970, Vol. 168) entitled *"Dying with Dignity"*.

"Marcus Aurelius' assertion that an emperor should die standing up and the Western pioneer's wish to die with his boots on, exemplify the desire to die with dignity. Increasingly we lose this opportunity. Progress in the prevention and cure of acute illness has shifted most deaths to the chronic disease category and has made lingering terminal illness more frequent. In earlier days, most people died at home or at work, tended by friends and family. Now the terminal patient has largely lost the security of dying in familiar surroundings, for most deaths occur in a hospital or nursing home, where medical skill and sophisticated equipment sometimes prolong vital signs after all hope of recovery and sometimes after sentience and self-control have disappeared. These capabilities are sometimes used, yet typically the treatment given the terminal patient is poorer in quality and quantity than that given the patient who is expected to recover, for the interest of the hospital staff is in sav-ing lives and restoring health. No member of the staff has had professional training in dealing with dying patients, their relatives, or the problems of bereavement. All of this makes for added stress for the patient and his family. One study has found that in the year following the death of one member of a family, the death rate among close relatives is twice as high if the primary death occurred in a hospital or nursing home, as it is if the primary death occurred at home. We have the curious situation that medical progress has made death more stressful for relatives, more expensive for the family, and more troublesome for society. Because these are discomforting matters, we have pushed them aside; death seems to have replaced sex as the socially taboo topic."

Now this paragraph covers a lot of territory, but I think we could begin with the last sentence, specifically, the observation that death discussions in our society are taboo. Or is there some sort of change we are now witnessing?

DR. STACEY DAY: That would be a good question for Bob Slater. However, he was rushed to the hospital, otherwise he might have opened this discussion very well. Let's ask a non-medical man. Mulford Sibley - why don't you start on that question!

PROFESSOR MULFORD SIBLEY: Well I think the attitude to death is changing very sharply. As a matter of fact, up till about six or seven years ago, I think this (quotation) would have been characteristic of American Society in a discussion of death as taboo. But, last year, I attended a conference on death sponsored by the Department of Sociology at Hamline University and it was packed. The interesting thing is that a high percentage of people who attended that conference were high school students and college students. So I believe that the ban on discussion of death is breaking down very much in contemporary American Society. It is not merely medical schools who are becoming concerned.

DR. STACEY DAY: B. J., you see a great deal of death, especially in the Cancer Unit and in fact daily on the wards. How would you answer this question?

DR. B. J. KENNEDY: The audience here demonstrates the fact that death is a very voguish subject. The physicians who deal with dying cancer patients, have, I think, been identified with the subject for a long time. We have been teaching about death a great number of years. With cancer patients, death and the disease have been interrelated. The subject of death itself has become of interest to everyone. A patient will frequently ask: "Am I going to die?" The usual answer that I will give is: *absolutely, I will guarantee all my patients that they will die.* It's surprising how a number of patients are amazed that a physician would say that they are going to die, maybe not today or tomorrow, but some day, and the willingness is there to talk with a patient who is interested in whether or not they are going to die. Death has been something that physicians did not talk about with their patients. As a result there was always a gap in communi-

cation between the doctor and the patient. In fact, it still exists where physicians don't always tell their patients the full situation and refrain from talking about the potential death of that specific patient.

At the University of Minnesota the Masonic Memorial Hospital was built as a "terminal cancer hospital." Actually, this meant a place to put patients with *recurrent* cancer. This hospital *has been* an environment in which death has been able to be discussed with nurses, house staff, faculty, social workers, orderlies and with the patient. This is what we deal with every day. Patients want to talk about death. There is no problem talking about death and I think what is happening with the public is they are learning that you *can* talk about death.

DR. STACEY DAY: Bob Fulton, you aren't a physician, yet I know you have been working in this area for a long time. You and people in your discipline, have given it an antiquated name; isn't it "Thanatology?" What are you going to say in answer to this question based on your long history of interest in death problems?

PROFESSOR ROBERT FULTON: We gave up the term "Thanatology" in favor of Death Education and Research several years ago, Stacey, in recognition of the fact that it reflected as much the bias of the culture as many of the other things that will probably be said here this afternoon. I think this audience tells us, and the one Professor Sibley was a

19

part of at Hamline tells us, that this is the first "death-free" generation in the history of the world - a generation that is being confronted with the question of longevity for what? You have two generations coming into conflict here; a generation that has, in its own private life, never really experienced death; and a generation of elderly people who constitute the largest and fastest growing population of elderly people this country has ever seen - 20 million, soon to be 25 million people. In terms of the Hipocratic Oath, these people constitute a group that must be kept alive, and must be assisted and aided in every way possible. The directive reads: "Primum non nocere" - first of all do no harm. So we are trapped at this particular time in our contemporary history with a generation that is very health oriented, very life oriented, very welfare oriented, and a generation that is most eligible to die. So I think one of the things that we see moving and pushing us is the questions regarding life for what? Longevity for what? Organ transplants for what? Extension of life for what? Extraordinary measures for what? When at the same time, according to all government statistics and reports, the elderly have very little to look forward to, regardless of how well their poor health might be. The segregation of the elderly and the abandonment and isolation of the elderly, raises fresh moral and ethical issues. Issues that have always been here, but, haven't been here in such a fashion. This is the point that I would make in commenting on Professor Kennedy's remarks. Of course we have always had death. I mean it is no more voguish than taxes. We have always had taxes too. We have always had death, but, we have never had it quite this way before. It has never been so private and so public at the same time in our history before, or in the history of any other society, for that matter. The point is not that death is voguish or death is new or something we are coming to recognize, instead, it is just that the whole sociological structure within which living and death occurs, has changed and changed profoundly. The various institutions and social groups and health care professionals are just now becoming aware of the situation, because, the stresses and strains within the various institutions are becoming intolerable for many, not the least of whom is the dying patient.

DR. STACEY DAY: Dick Simmons is our transplant surgeon. Dick, in you come and have a go!

DR. RICHARD SIMMONS: Is the discussion of death taboo? I think death is almost like sex. If we had had a sex conference we couldn't have driven in more people! Discussions of death are like sex - they are free and open to the public. You can watch it in a movie theatre, but discussing it with your children is slightly embarassing. In fact, it is more embarassing to discuss death with your children than it is to discuss sex, nowadays. Certainly it is with me and my family. There are lots of sssshhh around, particularly from the grandparents, when the problem of death comes up in the family. The other private realm of death is in the patient - death in the patient that you are taking care of is a very private matter. I think a doctor tends to not bring the subject up very often with the patient and when he does, he intellectualizes it, like we are doing here. For example, before transplantation, I always tell the patient his chances of dying in just so many words; "you have a 10% chance of dying one year following the operation tomorrow morning." I think this point is important for a patient to know, because he has a feeling that he is going to get this organ and by gosh he is going to run. He is not, and by at least pointing out to him that it is troublesome (that there are problems including death along the line) you give him and his family a more realistic attitude. I must say that I don't do that to my general surgical patients, where death is far less of a probability, because it is slightly embarassing to raise the possibility of failure. We, as physicians, do not like to contemplate failure. I think we are very embarassed by the idea of failure as physicians to our patients.

Dr. Stacey Day: John Brantner, would you like to add a post script?

Dr. John Brantner: I must say I agree with the observation that Bob Fulton has made. There is in our society a change and to answer the question about death - is it still a taboo subject? I think this is one of the most profound changes that has happened in our soci-

ety in the last five years or so. People are beginning to question the assumptions and the hypothesis on which we have based our lives. I think people are beginning to see that by ignoring death, by denying death, by closing it out from our consideration, we have done things that we didn't want to do about our lives. We are beginning to see that death underlies many of our moral questions, many of our political questions; so many things. Do we eat meat? If we do, perhaps we should examine this in the context that we are dining on death. Would we be willing to slaughter in order to eat meat? The question of vegetarianism or omnivorousness is one that involves death. We can not approach it intelligently and unemotionally if we exclude death from our consideration. This is perhaps a trivial example, but death pervades all the questions of war, the question of our traffic laws, the question of abortion and contraception. So many other things which are important to us now, can not be answered fully, unless we have made, as a society, a confrontation with death and we are beginning to realize this is true in individual lives. We are beginning to recognize the triviality that can enter into our lives if we draw a curtain somewhere around ourselves and refuse to consider what is going to happen to us in the years of our disability, the years of our old age, the time of our dying. If we are not able to make a confrontation with our own death, we are beginning to realize as a people that we lead trivial lives without this awareness. Kinnell,

Gaylord Kinnell a poet, said in one of his most recent poems that "living brings you to death - there are no other roads." I think there are many other indications as Bob knows better than I, which are intimations that we are coming to this realization. I think that's it.

DR. STACEY DAY: Thank you very much. Mark, may I have the next question?

MARK WOOD: I should say that several of these questions have been gathered from the medical student classes Phase A; Phase B. We will ask some of those questions and then Dr. Day will ask some of the questions that have been received by phone.

"How can a physician calm the fears of the dying patient? What can he say in terms of reassurance and guidance?"

DR. STACEY DAY: Let's give this to a non-physician first. Mulford Sibley, what would you say?

PROFESSOR MULFORD SIBLEY: Well I think I would tend to agree with what's already been said. One should be honest with a patient and tell him what his chances are of dying. At the same time, we can point out that all of us are slowly dying, as a matter of fact, almost from the very beginning of life. I guess I don't believe in compromise on things of this sort. I believe in frankness in a kindly way, I suppose, if you can combine frankness with consideration of feelings. These are the lines along which I suppose I would do it, however, I think a physician could answer it much better.

DR. STACEY DAY: John?

DR. JOHN BRANTNER: There are a couple of underlying questions in *that* question which I would like to raise and ask the physicians to respond. Are the dying afraid of dying? Are we often faced with the question? Are you often faced with the question of comforting the fears of the dying? Of given guidance?

DR. STACEY DAY: B. J., I think, is the best man on the panel to answer that particular question.

DR. B. J. KENNEDY: I think the question really relates to the beginning point when you are not ill. How many of you have considered that you are going to die? All of you *are*, but most of us here have the sort of plan that it is going to happen to *him* and *him* but not to me! This is the way of our society. We have not prepared our people for the fact that they really are going to die. However, the average person is a very courageous individual. When he is faced with a severe disease, which has the death implication, he has the ability to bring forth a tremendous amount of what the family will call courage. They comment on how courageous he is in facing his difficult problem. But I believe there is a tremendous capability for the average person to meet this phenomenon. He doesn't like the idea of dying and he doesn't want to be laden with a disease in which death is indicated. Faced with the disease and working with a physician who is able to discuss the disease and tell what he is going to do about it, the patient will, in time, adjust

22

very well to the aspect of dying and can realistically face that possibility.

It is very important that the physician who first works with the disease also be the same person who continues to take care of the patient totally, including the dying phase of the disease. Many times a change in clinics, or a change in physician looses a certain communication between the patient and the doctor. That is not as good as if the same physician dealt with the patient throughout the phase of dying. The patient will continue to fight his disease and try to avoid death. But once he understands that there is no possibility of recovery from his disease, he is able to adjust to death, if the physician is able to answer his questions and tell him what is coming. The patient doesn't want to know how he is going to be short of breath or the bloody details of the process of dying. What the patient wants to know is whether he or she is going to be uncomfortable during the phase of dying. This is where the physician can assure the patient that his comfort can be accomplished. A family is distressed, because in the process of watching someone die, things happen that are distressful to the family who have to observe the patient. These may not be distressful to the patient. The impending impact of death and the fact that it can be very beautiful, is illustrated by studies of patients where they were in the process of drowning and literally almost dead and then recovered. Or in other medical circumstances, where they went through the process of dying but didn't actually die. They do not find that this was a distressful circumstance. In a sense, it is bad for us to watch a patient die, but the *actual process* is not difficult. Hence a physician can work with the patient. He doesn't have to promise things that he is not going to be able to deliver, but by realistically and honestly working with the patient, I think that a patient can die in dignity, and comfortably. Many patients in a certain phase of illness reach a point where they want to die. We don't conceive an ultimate goal of keeping ourselves living eternally and we really can be happy with the idea that death is imminent.

DR. STACEY DAY: Thank you B.J. I am going to move on because there are so many questions and we could, I think, spend an hour on each. I am going to ask Mark Wood to pull a question out of the euthanasia bag and I am going to give this first to Bob Fulton. The question is: "*Birth is no longer blindly accepted but increasingly is planned and timed. Does this development and growing acceptance of abortion indicate a readiness to consider Euthanasia?*" I don't know about that one. I think you need a philosopher. Bob, you go ahead.

PROFESSOR ROBERT FULTON: We have several philosophers on this panel, I am sure. Some of you are acquainted with the second world war gold stars that used to hang in the windows of many homes across this country. The impulse toward Euthanasia is growing so fast and so strong that I wouldn't be a bit surprised that within this decade, the decade that I have labelled "The Decade of Death", the young people of America will be putting up such stars in the windows of their homes across the country with the slogan "We Gave." It will be their parents or their grandparents who were "given." This is a two generational society. Life expectancy is 70.5 years. 70 years ago it was 47 years. We will have 25 million people over 65 at the end of the decade and they are the most eligible to die. Almost 8 million people are over 75. 20,000 people are over a century old. We don't know what to do with them. We have no place for them. As I say, the society has changed so profoundly that for most of them, they are economically obsolete. They are sociologically obsolete. In terms of the change of family structure of American Society, they are obsolete as family members. They are separated and isolated, psychologically if not physically from their family, simply by virtue of the fact that this is a youth oriented society - a two generational society. Yet we have a four generational population, demographically it is four generational and we don't know what to do. So what has been suggested in England - having had a second reading in the House of Parliament - is a bill giving the right to a patient to request of a doctor that he kill him. The whole question of the right to die, to take one's own life when he so chooses, when he is no longer, in his terms, willing to accept the conditions of his life, is becoming more and more acceptable

to the American public all the time. John Berryman was to have been on this program and his name was prominently displayed on the brochure and the various bulletins throughout the campus. But, on our bulletin board, his name was crossed out by some student and was written in that he had died waving goodby and that was his last existential act. That is the only comment that I have had from any of my colleagues or any of my students with respect to Professor Berryman's death. The right to take one's own life, as I say, is popular among the young, acceptable to us, growing in acceptability, because we look to the elderly to commit that act for us and solve many of the ethical and moral problems that at the present time are beyond our capabilities.

PROFESSOR MULFORD SIBLEY: May I ask a question in that connection? Do you personally approve of Euthanasia? You have been describing the tendency and I wondered whether you would be willing to state your own view on that point?

PROFESSOR ROBERT FULTON: No I don't.

PROFESSOR MULFORD SIBLEY: I don't either.

DR. STACEY DAY: John Brantner, what have you got to say about that point? I would like you to limit your comments, because I would like to get through as many questions as possible. I don't want to close you up, of course, because these questions are extremely interesting, but please give shorter, snappier answers so we can get through more questions. John.

DR. JOHN BRANTNER: It is coming. Many of us in this room will be faced with the question of deciding for ourselves, under which conditions, legally and appropriately, not feloniously or any such thing, is life acceptable to us. I hope we will never be faced, any of us in this room, with the question that has been posed under the context of Euthanasia - involuntary Euthanasia - under what conditions is life acceptable for others. We are thinking of voluntary statutory euthanasia. It will come. Many of us will be faced with this question. We will have to ask ourselves the very, very basic fundamental question - under what conditions is life acceptable to me? When is death an acceptable event in my life? And there is another question lying behind that we will then face. What are the appropriate conditions of death. If we decide we are eligible for death and death has become an acceptable outcome, what is a solution at this stage. For those in the whole Health Care business, the "appropriateness of death" is a basic question. How should people die under those circumstances? It relates very directly, the right to die, voluntary euthanasia not only to the question of asking my physician to cease medical treatment but asking him to kill me since I am unable to kill myself under many of the conditions that I would define. And reserving for myself, the right to kill myself. I would also express my *personal* belief: I see this coming. I suppose I am willing to defend it as a right for others. I can conceive of no circumstances under which I would avail myself of this right.

DR. STACEY DAY: Dick Simmons, let us say that you open me up say, in the operating room, and find I have an inoperable cancer. I tell you that I wish to die. What are you going to say to me? Is this a request for what we call "euthanasia?" What will you tell me?

DR. RICHARD SIMMONS: In one sense we already have euthanasia. A patient can refuse further treatment, and some patients choose to do just that. If you will point out to him what his chances are of having such and such an operation, a number of hemodialysis patients, for example, will say this is not acceptable and will not accept further hemodialysis treatment or immuno-suppressive treatment for transplantation, or chemotherapy for cancer. The patient will withhold treatment and go elsewhere. I don't know any physician whose experience is likely to be otherwise, except in the case of children, when parents make the decision for them (we had one case). Even there it is difficult to go to the courts. I think that this is an important thing. Euthanasia, in that sense, has already arrived.

DR. STACEY DAY: Do you think it desirable for society to pass some sort of legislation which would give a panel of physicians, not the right, but the possibility of making a judgement value on whether life should be terminated? For society as a whole, would that be a desirable or a non-desirable thing from the point of view of a physician?

DR. RICHARD SIMMONS: It would not be desirable for society to make that kind of a decision. They have made it in a sense in abortion, which is prenatal infanticide. It is a social decision that has been made to go ahead with abortion, but not post-natal infanticide.

DR. STACEY DAY: Fine. Now I want to ask one other question that occurs to me and I want to put it to Mulford Sibley. I imagine that he as a political scientist is dealing with historical science, in a sense, and is dealing with another aspect of death that I want to get into this symposium - and that is *mass* death. So far we have been discussing what I might call the death of the individual. Most of the questions have been individualizing death. But how about the situation where one drops a bomb or some sort of obliterating mechanism which can wipe out millions of people? Do the principles, the philosophy we have been discussing - do these things apply to the death of *whole* societies, *whole cities,* or is that a different kettle of fish? War, death in war; is it the same problem or is it another?

PROFESSOR MULFORD SIBLEY: Well I think you have raised a very basic question. The 20th century has been characterized by polarization (saving of individual lives, so to speak, by medical science) but, also on the other hand, by mass deaths not only in war but production of refugees, the deliberate obliteration of whole peoples. Whole nations are involved in this. From one point of view, the individual can only die once. It doesn't make any difference whether he dies in an act of war or in some other respect, but, I suppose from the social viewpoint, quite often the spectacle of mass death has a much more profound effect on us than dying one by one. Ethically, I see no distinction between deliberate killing in private lives and deliberate killing in war. Both are in the same category, in my judgement. Also, let me make a quick observation on abortion and euthanasia. At least this can be said for voluntary euthanasia, that the person has a voice in his own death, he is deciding about it, he is making a judgement, but when we commit an act of abortion the fetus has no say in whether he is going to die. I think there is an important distinction here.

DR. STACEY DAY: Thank you very much. I have three questions now, of which I am going to ask one each to a separate member of the panel. I am going to start with B. J. "*Do you have any sugtestions on how to develop a healthy realistic attitude toward death?*"

DR. B. J. KENNEDY: I think the average person must, in his own judgement, begin to decide what is his purpose in living; what his goals are, and then accept the realistic fact that some day he will die. In so doing, when he is faced with the reality of death, it will not be as traumatic to him as it is to the person who has totally blinded himself to the fact that death is going to occur. Forming a will is a very good illustration that he accepts the fact he is going to die.

DR. STACEY DAY: Thank you B. J.. John Brantner, *"How do you view your own death? Do you ever think about it?"*

DR. JOHN BRANTNER: Following B. J.'s advice, I think about it daily. As a deliberate discipline. I would carry that advice farther. Rather, I would recommend, or list, some practical means of carrying out the kind of confrontation with your own death. Not only with your own death, but also with your own disability, the planning for disaster and death. Regardless of how much we think of this, how much we try to confront our own, when it arrives, when the news of it arrives, it is going to be seen by us as a disaster. But we can prepare for disaster. We can consider - those of us who wear spectacles - what we will do in those days when we can not read? We can anticipate our own paraplegia, our own strokes. We can make this blow less in that we will have given it thought. I think this is one of the keys for death. Think about it daily. In the context of your prayers, your meditations, while brushing your teeth, at some regular time whatever, think about it daily. Accustom yourself to looking at your possessions and your relationships with others in this context. On parting from another, remind yourself, not in a morbid gloomy way, but in a way that may catch you up in a quarrel, or catch you up in hasty words, that this may be the last parting from this person. Never consciously part from another if you can work it without that thought flitting through your head. Each encounter with another may be the last encounter you have with this person. Wandering, as I have often recommended, through your rooms saying, as you look at your possessions maybe once a day, "There is nothing here that isn't going to have to be disposed of by somebody else someday." Also, I would strongly recommend the thing that has become repugnant to most people. I think this repugnance, or shall I say, our *reluctance* to do this, would be greatly improved if we did just that. I think people should also attend funerals when they are not, themselves, the central mourners. I think this would have two effects. One, it would improve funerals if we attended when we were not, ourselves, blind with grief. Secondly, I think that the funeral is a great institution for instruction in mourning. We don't need to be taught how to grieve, we need to learn how to mourn - to mourn efficiently, mourn effectively, to do our grief work, and in our mourning, to re-enter life. The funeral is a good way to let us see what we can expect in ourselves and what happens to other people in this way.

DR. STACEY DAY: I will go on to Bob Fulton who knows most, I think, about this next question. *"Do you feel Americans have a special way of approaching death?"* I think this is a very good question. Having spent time in the east (India) and in other countries, and remembering aspects of these cultures, such as the Kamikaze pilots of the last war, the immolation of Bhuddist monks, and other similar death acts, I feel there is definitely a cultural attitude toward death. What would you say about this question? Do you feel Americans have a special way of approaching death?

PROFESSOR ROBERT FULTON: I think it is regrettable, the set of attitudes that have developed. Now you will not believe this because most of you are medical people, but I have had graduate students and graduate nurses, in my seminar on Death, Grief and Bereavement, *who have never seen a dead human body!* Now you say that is physically and professionally impossible. Not if you close your eyes! This girl is here and presumably practicing. She is here at this hospital. She will remain anonymous of course, but you will appreciate the fact that she has gone through the nursing program and has never seen a dead human body. This kind of experience is the lifetime experience of most of us in the privatization of death. The longevity of our citizens, the isolation of the elderly, the movement toward memorialization and privatization of death and the ready disposal of bodies, and so on, all contribute. Removal of the dead from the home, the chronically ill from the home, and finally the elderly from the home, are phenomena that occurred in just 50 years in this country. It makes me nervous to come here when I think and remember that of the two million people who will die this year, over 2/3 of them will die in a hospital. Over 2/3 of them are over 65. We have no experience

with death-and death is really the medical practitioners' problem. To that extent the few little statistics that I can throw out tell us of a unique cultural experience that people throughout the rest of the world have yet to experience.

DR. STACEY DAY: Thank you Bob. I am going to give this question to Dick Simmons. There are three, actually, I would like to give him, but I think I will choose this one. I guess a Medical Student asked this question. *"Am I pledged to maintain existence in all my patients? Must I initiate procedures which will keep ventilation, circulation going when I know that each day of existence depletes the material reserves of the family, uses up valuable economic resources, and offers no chance for the patient to again enjoy a normal life."* I think every surgical resident has seen a patient come in with traumatic shock from a motor car accident. Fluids are pumped in, everything that we can possibly give is pumped in, and, yet, I imagine that everybody in the team knows that he is probably not going to survive. I think this is a very important question. Dick what are you going to say?

DR. RICHARD SIMMONS: With respect to other members of the panel, whom I hope will remain my friends, it sounds like death is a desirable thing; personally I think death is not very desirable. It may be socially desirable and it may be ecologically important for society, but it is not a desirable thing for the person involved. Should one do everything possible to save that heart beating, presumably brain living cadaver? The answer is yes, even if you think otherwise, because you will be wrong on occasion. As long as you really think there is a possibility of continuing existence, recovery is possible. I think there is an overstated point in the Science Magazine, which was obviously not written by a physician, that there is dignity in dying. I don't see that it is very dignified. Death is no more nor less dignified on a respirator than it is falling in the middle of the street in a car accident. I think the patient deserves an attempt to save his life. On the other hand, when failure to save his life has occurred, he also deserves to be made as comfortable as possible and that death be as quick as possible without euthanasia. Thus, some rational decisions must be made. Perhaps transplantation has helped make those decisions by deciding when brain death has occurred. You can decide when brain death has occurred and turn off the respirator, even if the organs are not going to be used for somebody else. I don't think it is in fact a really difficult decision in medical practice.

DR. STACEY DAY: Mulford Sibley, I want you to add a postscript on that question because you are not a medical man. Would you add another point of view? In point of fact, is the physician pledged to maintain existence in all patients irrespective of the fact that the reserve - presumably financial reserve - of the patient is used up as may be all of his economic feasabilities?

PROFESSOR MULFORD SIBLEY: In general yes. I should offer a distinction between doing something positively to cause the death of a patient and simply not doing anything to prolong life. I think there is an important distinction between those two. I don't know what a physician would say, but I would make a distinction.

DR. STACEY DAY: Anybody else want to say anything in response to this question?

DR. JOHN BRANTNER: I think the question suggests that the patient's ability to pay for treatment is important in the decision - that is nonsense.

DR. STACEY DAY: B. J., then to follow up I will ask if Bob Fulton has any experience. Professor B. J., *"Are most deaths tranquil?"* I don't know whether one can generalize on such a thing as death, but that was the question. *"Are most deaths tranquil?"*

DR. B. J. KENNEDY: I would like to think that those under my care are.

DR. STACEY DAY: That's very sweet. Let's pass this on to Bob Fulton. In your experiences and I know you have traveled the world in many, many countries, picking up data on cultural and anthropological death, would you say, in your experience, most deaths are tranquil?

PROFESSOR ROBERT FULTON: Only if your enemies are dead! I would concur with Richard and Professor Kennedy that this is a multifaceted question. I don't think any of us want to die - and the dying least of all. But there are many problems between the dying patient and the physician, between the dying patient and the nursing staff. The question raises the specter of the relationship of the dying patient to his relatives, to his friends, and survivors to say nothing of his wife and girl friend. All of these things have to be considered by and for us all.

DR. STACEY DAY: Thank you. I am going to move on from here. I am going to give a personal experience. Not long ago a friend of mine, a Greek, came to me and posed the question of a colleague of his who was dying of leukemia. His problem was that his friend was dying and that daily, large troops of physicians and students and all sorts of people would march into the room and discuss the patient in terms of his electrolytes, and his physiologic status and everything else. Nobody, it appeared, seemed to think that the patient still had an intellect. Obviously, in many diseases, and in chronic diseases, we are faced with a patient who is dying in body, but sound in intellectual mind and I want to raise this problem and throw it out to you. I want you to incorporate that sort of thinking in this question and I imagine you can with a little bit of ingenuity. This further question says, *"What are the most important concerns of the patient in preparing for his or her death? Physical comfort? they ask you. Emotional stability? they ask you. Personal and family obligations? they ask you. Loneliness?"* Who am I going to give this to first. Lets see, Dick Simmons.

DR. RICHARD SIMMONS: It depends on what category of patient you are describing. In the acutely ill young patient, I think the greatest concern is that he hopes like crazy that everybody around him is trying to prevent death. Therefore, I do not object in the slightest (in fact we tell all our patients that we will) to standing at the bedside and discussing the technological problems with them so they can raise their head and say, "that's not right, I didn't vomit this morning." I think you can approach the problem better and I think it also reinforces him that you are very, very concerned and doing your damnest to make him better. The patient for whom death is inevitable may require much more emotional stability and support. With that I have not really had a lot of experience.

DR. STACEY DAY: B. J., you see this situation in cancer patients I am sure.

DR. B. J. KENNEDY: I think the first requirement is that the physician, who is caring for a patient in the process of dying, must be a compassionate individual. If he is not, he is not really ready to take care of the dying patient. Talking before a patient is permissible, but I believe it is very important that the conversation be translated into the patients' own intelligence level so he understands what the scientific language really means to him. If he hears a lot of words including that of death, or operation, or other key words, his anxiety level will be increased. He needs to have translation and interpretation. It is important that each patient have *one* doctor who is the captain of the team, to be able to translate what the scientific terminology really means. It is conflicting and disturbing to a patient to have five translations by five different people, because the translation always comes out differently. It is important that the team captain be the translator. The patient at all levels, be he not very intelligent or very intelligent, has a concept of what death is, what it might be. For this patient you have to work with him so he has an understanding of the problem.

DR. STACEY DAY: The last one that I will ask is John Brantner, because he is a clinical psychologist and I think might contribute something to that question.

DR. JOHN BRANTNER: I would say that the most important thing, at least from the point of view of the psychologist who is concerned with some of the interior aspects of human life under all conditions of life, is disability. The dying should be permitted and indeed encouraged to negotiate with his environment for the satisfaction of his own needs and he should be seen as a person even under these conditions. With life lasting only minutes or days, yet he is a person who has significant growth to accomplish. If this is the way his environment is interacting with him, all of the other things are irrelevancies.

DR. STACEY DAY: Thank you John. Now I think we will deviate from the fixed program. We have about ten more minutes left and if these discussions are

to be audience participatory, I think the best thing is to throw this meeting open to the audience at large, to ask questions. One or two of you should come up and ask your questions and we will get the panel to give their answers to as many questions as can be done with short fast answers. So, if any of you want to ask questions, why don't you come up now.

AUDIENCE QUESTIONER: One of the questions you raised was with regard to the physician making a judgement on the basis of medical knowledge, determining whether or not a patient should live. Obviously this is a very ethical question. A comment was made about having a panel of physicians make a judgement as to whether or not life should be prolonged. I am kind of concerned that the non-physician and non-medical students are part of a broad society which *should* be concerned because these questions are of an ethical nature and not purely medical.

DR. STACEY DAY: Well let's give this observation to a non-physician. Mulford Sibley why don't you comment.

PROFESSOR MULFORD SIBLEY: I think he is exactly right that questions of technical medicine ought to be distinguished from ethical questions and we all have a right and an obligation to discuss the ethical dimension of all these issues. Even when we don't have technical knowledge, for example, in the field. On abortion and euthanasia and so on, the physician can assist us, it seems to me, in providing the connecting link between the ethical problem and the particular issue involved. But, the two issues should be, I think, distinguished.

DR. STACEY DAY: Bob Fulton, you are not a physician. Why don't you answer that question from your point of view?

PROFESSOR ROBERT FULTON: Well, very briefly. I think we obviously appreciate the fact that we do have two physicians on the panel who are aware of two things: that dying is a human process and that death is a social event. I think essentially what Mulford is saying, as well as John, is that we are dealing here with critical issues, critical social and ethical issues that also happen to be in our generation medical issues. It is a matter of sifting out and arranging in this last half of the 20th century the answers to these very complex and difficult questions.

DR. STACEY DAY: Are there any other questions?

AUDIENCE MEMBER: Would physicians on the panel please amplify what they mean by "failure" as a cause of death in their patients.

DR. RICHARD SIMMONS: We do make mistakes but I didn't want to say so. The hang up is that I just happen to be a surgeon who mentioned death. I mean, I think you have to tell a patient, as part of this therapy, if he is going to have a hernia fixed, that there is a possibility that he is going to die, but his chances of dying are about one in a thousand. I think we do not spell out this possibility, that is one in one thousand. In the transplant patient, I never soften it and

I really spell it out because the chances are so much greater, and death becomes a very real possibility to him and his family. It's not that it's a mistake, it's a failure. Failure to prolong life is a failure of medicine in a sense. It is a failure in our job. It may not be our fault that it's a failure, but it is a failure.

DR. B. J. KENNEDY: The failure on the part of science that it is not good enough to prevent what is happening is *not* a personal failure on *your* part. You perform as best as science can provide. When science can't provide a total cure or even limited health, then the role of the physician is to help the patient die.

AUDIENCE MEMBER: But isn't there more of a cultural label to say that death is a phase of dying?

DR. JOHN BRANTNER: Then you get into the thing that B. J. mentioned at the beginning. All of his patients die, therefore, if you really followed this you are in a profession which fails in 100% of its efforts.

DR. B. J. KENNEDY: To my patients who say, "Am I going to die", I absolutely guarantee it. All of my patients die and if you find a doctor who tells you otherwise, I wouldn't trust him. It is a nice introduction for a patient and the doctor to start talking about death.

DR. STACEY DAY: I am going to close now with one last question. There are a large number of people here I think who are classified as hospital personnel. Perhaps it may be said that much of our attitude has been stressed in terms of professional approach, particularly for the student, but when a patient dies in a hospital there are many other people who come into contact with that patient besides the physician. Everyone is familiar with ward nurses crying when a young child dies because there is obviously some empathic relationship between the people who treat the child and the child. Being physicians, one sees janitors with tears in their eyes, or a floor sweeper crying when a particular patient dies, because again of some empathic relationship. I am going to ask each of you in turn, even if you are not physicians, to give me a little comment, maybe a minute each, on how you think the relationship or the expression of the so called hospital personnel, in terms of death, is related with the question of death. The janitor on the floor, he who probably cleans the windows, the man who trundles in the stretcher; all these are part of our hospital set up and how should they take part in this process of death? I am going to start with John Brantner.

DR. JOHN BRANTNER: Simply to quote Donne: "Every man's death diminishes me." In so far as my life overlaps with any other, I will respond with grief and I will mourn. In the context of the hospital, I think this should be encouraged. We don't have time to talk at great length as we might next week. I think this kind of involvement should be encouraged - personal involvement, concern, becoming personally involved with our patients on all levels, the things we have been frightened of for so many

years. One consequence of this is that depending on how greatly our lives have overlapped with the person who is dying, we feel grief and we will all of us mourn.

DR. STACEY DAY: Bob Fulton do you have some comments?

PROFESSOR ROBERT FULTON: I definitely concur and would just repeat what I said before. Death is a social event and just as if the head surgeon expects everyone in the operating room to be privy to the fact that bacteria are everywhere and that death and disease is possible and that everyone, everyone who is concerned with the patient to be operated upon, must be no less aware, so too I think with respect to anybody who comes into contact with the dying patient. That his death and the problems associated with it is of concern not only to himself and to his family, but also to the medical staff and so on. His death at some level of experience will be shared by everyone.

DR. STACEY DAY: Dick?

DR. RICHARD SIMMONS: I have nothing to add.

DR. STACEY DAY: B. J.?

DR. B. J. KENNEDY: Death is a loss. I think everybody will experience it among the hospital personnel. The degree of loss is relative, probably related to the direct contact with the dying patient. I think the greatest loss comes to the nurses. They have been closely taking care of the patient. Some very special relationships develop. You may see a whole floor be emotionally crushed, because one patient has died.

DR. STACEY DAY: Mulford, Do you have any thinking on this?

PROFESSOR MULFORD SIBLEY: Well, it seems to me part of a broader question with which we began this panel, specifically, between impersonalism in death, in this society, which seems to want to reduce a person to a thing, and personalism. There is far too much of the first attitude and it is a constant battle to keep from being reduced simply to a thing. And I think that if a hospital employee or anyone else feels a sense of empathy it should be encouraged. It is really a saving grace that so many people still care enough to feel deeply when the whole tendency of the culture, in many respects, is in the other direction.

DR. STACEY DAY: That is a very fine conclusion for this particular meeting. I thank every member of the panel and Mark Wood and the Student Council. I hope we can reconvene next week to continue. Thank you very, very much indeed.

Death – The Physician,
The Patient, Hospital
Personnel and Relatives

DR. JAMES SCHLESS: Today, again, we have Dr. Day, the Conservator of the Bell Museum of Pathology, as the moderator. The medical student representative from the student council remains Mark Wood. We have a new and welcome voice, Regent Loanne Thrane, who will represent some very interesting points of view. We have also Chaplain Neil Hering who is the House Chaplain for the University of Minnesota Hospitals. We again held over for a second showing, Dr. John Brantner, Professor of Clinical Psychology and Dr. Dick Simmons, Associate Professor of Surgery. A new addition is Dr. Ignacio Fortuny, Associate Professor of Medicine and Director of the Medicine and Cancer Tutorial Program. We have Professor Robert Slater who is director of Mortuary Sciences and I think to this

group at least the last participant hardly needs any introduction, Regents' Professor of Pediatrics and Microbiology and Chairman of the Department of Pathology, Dr. Bob Good. Stacey it's yours.

DR. STACEY DAY: Thank you Jim. We are trying to create a conceptual climate for the student body to arrive at possible resolutions to the questions it has raised and that we try to answer with you. Now last week we dealt with questions of cultural attitudes and changing attitudes toward death. The panel raised and answered, to some degree, the so called question of taboo on discussion on death and its effect on our society. Other problems that were taken up were aspects of euthanasia, including the patient's right to voluntarily request the ending of his life. Some other perspectives discussed moral and political aspects of death, such matters as whether society prepares the individual to face death and especially his own death and we had some interesting answers on that subject. We also discussed attitudes toward death en masse as in war and whether such death was distinct in its attitude from death of the individual. We shall go on from there.

MARK WOOD: In order to help the panel I have divided the questions into three general areas. We shall continue with discussion of the patient, then we will get into the reaction of the family and then bereavement and funerals.

DR. STACEY DAY: Fine. The first question is for Loanne. *"What is the greatest help to the dying patient? Faith in religion? Confession of guilt? Putting affairs in order? Honest and real interpersonal communication? A loving family?"*

REGENT THRANE: I guess I must preface my remarks by saying that I am speaking as an individual possibly with a woman's interpretation. I think it is impossible to react to just one of those as being the most important. Certainly as an individual, religious faith would rank at the very top, but, I think also it is important that you have the sensitivity of your family and understanding of your family backing you. A feeling of concern, the fact that they have sympathy for you. Sympathy is certainly important. I also think that putting your affairs in order, so to speak, would have a priority.

DR. STACEY DAY: Fine ma'am. I am sure

Dr. Bob Good will carry on. What would you say would be the greatest help to the dying—all or one?

DR. ROBERT GOOD: I think all are important, but I am not sure if any are the most crucial thing. I think the most important thing in helping the dying patient is reassurance based on genuine friendship and compassion. A truly sympathetic person, particularly one in whom the patients can give complete confidence, can really help a patient by giving his approval of death and reassurance when a dying patient must accept a new adventure. A physician who is also a friend and confidant can often do the most in this regard. A close friend, even a member of the family, can fill this essential role. The role is one of helping the person through death. Telling him in one way or another that everything is being done, all has been done, often not much need be said, simply a touch of the hand, a simple and understanding and accepting look may be what is needed. From my own recent experience with death, my own feeling that I had been deprived of the opportunity to help in this way, added remorse and even guilt to my sorrow. I was in Europe when my aged mother died. It really bothered me that I had not been at home to help my mother start her journey in peace. We had faced death many times and very directly in open discussions of her deepest philosophies, fears, desires for completion of her life and anticipation of what was to come. I am sure that kind of preparation was helpful. Even though we like to say that everyone must die alone is not and I think should not be the case. I had the feeling that mother would have welcomed help from me in this regard. A quiet reassuring word, a touch of the hand symbolizing that it is all right now to die. It seems to me this role can be one of the most important for a physician in helping a patient face death. Although it is a role that often falls to the physician, it can be played equally well by a family member, close friend, sympathetic nurse. It is one of the real reasons we need conferences of this sort, that we need much thought about death. To be reassuring, the physician, family member, friend, nurse or attendant, must themselves have a degree of security about death and willingness when it is inevitable, to face it directly and not run away or avoid the direct and sympathetic confrontation.

DR. STACEY DAY: Ignacio, how would you answer that question?

DR. IGNACIO FORTUNY: I would emphasize that like everything in life, it is our *behavior* to dying and death that is important and, of course, I am speaking of my own experience with death which is dealing with the cancer patient, facing of the dying process, and finally the event of death. I find that as Dr. Good says, it is very important to have this approval which translated to "it's all right", means to me my behavior toward my loved one. Dying puts us at peace by leveling, in circumstances, what in the past may have been differences between us. Then if we can talk about those dif-

ferences and get in the realm of saying "you are all right and I am all right and, therefore, from now on we can go on together and I will be at your side with no pity, but with real understanding and concern for you." That to me is the best way to help a loved one die. And certainly, too, we have to think that death leaves the family in bereavement and this is the way I think one as a doctor can guide people to deal with their own grief and be left with only sadness at the end. That is the best way I can define death for myself, living with the void of a person you love, but with no regrets and no guilts after that person has gone.

DR. STACEY DAY: Thank you very much. Chaplain Hering.

CHAPLAIN HERING: I guess I really wouldn't divorce or make into separate categories, each one of those either. I would say that a person's religious faith, their relationship to their Lord, gives a meaning in that it enables them to feel free enough to be open and genuine in their relationships with their own family and with each other. In this way, there might be an honesty and a comfortableness with each other, as comfortable as you can possibly be, in dying and at death. Death can intensify guilt and isolation. Through their being accepted-then the dying person and his family can hopefully break through the guilt that could keep them alone from each other.

DR. STACEY DAY: John Brantner.

DR. JOHN BRANTNER: All of these are

reflections of what might be looked upon as one central fact of life, not only when faced with your own death, faced with loss through death of someone you love, faced with disability, faced with all the horrors that life can bring. If we are going to get through life and do a decent job of getting through life, we must have some sort of sources of hope, reassurance and trust indeed. All of these are reflections of the same thing. Somehow, from religious faith, from trust in physicians that everything is going to be done medically, from having (I hope) long before this, put all of the affairs in order, from knowing that your relationships with your family are fine, you know, basically, that no matter what happens, everything is going to be all right. And from whatever source they come, I see all of these as reflections of that central fact, of a trust indeed, which can come from all of these. But basically to face the terror, chaos, darkness - all of the horror that life can bring, and feel still the basic and perhaps primitive fundamental trust-in-being: everything is going to be all right, even so. What Will James called a hundred years ago "the yea-sayers to life," the ones who standing on the abyss will say to life "Yes, I will have it even so." All of these are reflections of the same fundamental trust-in-being, even in death.

DR. STACEY DAY: Thank you John. Now it is very good to have with us Bob Slater from the Mortuary Science Division - because I think this is one of the areas where interpersonal relations and inter-personal communications, especially at the family level, are important. Let's hear how you would answer that one Bob Slater?

PROFESSOR ROBERT SLATER: I think that the answers that have been given are such that no one would argue with them. I picked up where Dr. Good made the statement that it is important for the patient to know that it is all right to die. I think at the moment of death we must grant that same privilege to those who survive the deceased. They live in our ambivalent culture which seems to say in many ways that if you are going to do anything as unpatriotic as to die, don't do it around me. I will put you in a special home. I will put you in a special city or if you would like to take a long trip and not come back that is all right with me. The family has to be told, even as the patient, you are now in grief, you are in bereavement, and it is OK. Centuries, in fact all ages have recordings of rights of passage at the time of death, and these have been developed to work out these strong feelings. We no longer require people to stay home a year or to wear a black arm band, as if to say you are contagious stay away from me until the incubation period is over.

We have to let people know that they have entered a new experience. They have invested emotional capital in a person. That person's life is ended and in the process they have to withdraw that investment not only to re-invest it, but to be able to live with themselves, as the chaplain said, without the guilt and some of the fear that goes with it.

DR. STACEY DAY: Thank you very much. Now Dick Simmons I haven't forgotten you, but in order to move through a series of questions (and all these questions are so interesting) I am going to swing questions around the panel, varying things, so that we don't get you all answering the same question. I am going to group together two questions for you Dick. *"Do most patients know when they are dying?"* I want to add a rider to that which actually is another question, *"does the patient too often fall into the mutual conspiracy of silence with his doctor when facing death?"*

DR. RICHARD SIMMONS: Yes, I think the patient does know when he is dying, at least for a brief moment. If you deal with acute illness, there is a moment in which you, as a physician, feel intense anxiety and it is when the patient is slipping out of hand. You can usually see the anxiety written on the patient's face too. In that acute period of anxiety when he is denying that he is ill, and then all of a sudden slips in the anxiety of dying, it is very intense. You never know what to do and they never know what to do. Usually that period is followed very briefly by a coma or absence of consciousness, which is perhaps fortunate. During chronic illness I think the patients know and suspect they are ill. Psychologists have described the pattern of responses, defense mechanisms. Perhaps Dr. Brantner would rather call them something else, in which you deny, then you feel anxious, and then you make some kind of adaptation to your own death; I think, this,

they all feel. They are in the hospital to get well and they know the opposite of getting well is death and this is an extremely anxiety provoking experience for a while.

DR. STACEY DAY: *"Does the patient fall into a conspiracy of silence?"* I actually like that phrase. A mutual conspiracy of silence with his doctor when facing death?

DR. RICHARD SIMMONS: Yes I think most patients fall into a "conspiracy of silence". In acute illness, you have to actively bring up the subject of death to them. The patients are in the hospital to prevent death. They really are, in a sense, denying the reality of death when they come to the hospital because they come to get well. They overcome the denial to a degree when they do come. It is like going to the dentist for me. They don't want to face up to the fact that there is something wrong because it is going to be painful, and uncomfortable, and expensive to get it done. When you finally make the admission that there is something wrong, you will go to the Doctor but you still won't raise the question of death. As Dr. Kennedy said last week, he is happy when the patient asks "Am I going to die" because he knows how to deal with it and he knows the patient needs it dealt with. The patient, however, doesn't always ask, or it takes a long time for him to ask.

DR. STACEY DAY: Thank you very much. Dr. Bob Good, the same question.

DR. ROBERT GOOD: Well I think there are a number of aspects I would like to bring out. First of all I think that physicians dealing with the issue of death, and perhaps Dr. Simmons indicated this in his own discussion, really are afraid to deal with this question. Because they fear death. Physicians, of course, do not fear death in their patients for the same reason the patient himself fears death. We often fear death for a very special reason. From their earliest childhood, we have often been selected and rewarded by that selection. Our mothers often times have initiated the selection process by selecting us as the favorite son who will be a doctor some day. We have been selected all through school as successes, successful students-the top of the heap, the cream of the milk. We come to feel that we are sort of omnipotent from the perspective as the great healer and in the modern outlook of medicine, to face death of his patient, for a physician, is often facing failure, the physician's failure, his inability to cope successfully. He fears this and shies from it. He sometimes even blames the patient. As a clinician we see this view of failure in the implied criticism of our fellows, we see it in our isolation of the dying patients. If we can get plenty of machinery and resuscitative personnel in the way, the responsibility does not seem so immediate. As a pathologist, for reasons related to quality control and hopefully growth of the knowledge and profession, we must face physician's failures, mistakes, and omissions daily and we see this fear in another way. One of the most difficult things is to persuade the busy physician of the importance of presenting his case to the pathologist in the morgue - of even coming to the autopsy room to consider his patient in death. You see the patient's death represents to the physician his failure. As one approaching omnipotence, it is difficult to face the death of his patient directly. Visits to the autopsy room by physicians, if they come at all these days, are perfunctory and lacking reflection. In this symposium, we have been hearing the expression of a delightful development. We are trying to look at death in every perspective and in doing this should be helping the physician help his patient deal with death. So often the physician, having trouble thinking about death himself, doesn't look at death from the patient's perspective at all. In asking himself whether he should discuss the patient's impending death with the patient, the physician as often as not is asking himself whether he, himself, by now, has the courage to face his own failure, his inadequacy. He is not asking himself how he can best help his patient face the issue of the latter's death. Death comes so differently. It comes in so many different ways. With chronic illness, it often comes in several stages. First as an acquaintance, then as a brief visitor, later as a persistent visitor and watcher and finally as a bedfellow thoroughly accepted and perhaps a real partner to the patient. The physician at each stage may have to play a very different role in helping the patient deal with the intruder. He may, at first, be mainly called upon to help the patient and family think of keeping the "intruder" away, hopefully for a long time. He may later need to reassure the patient that he recognizes and accepts what the patient sees, but that he can do much to delay the progressive steps in the relationship and any unpleasantness of the progression of the relationship. Finally his role may be one of reassurance. The intruder is here, even intimately and immediately here, but, it is not so bad; indeed it is all right. If the physician has been willing to accept death himself, he can often be most helpful in facing the stages of death. He won't discuss death openly and traumatically when it is unnecessary. When the patient already knows he is going to die it is useless to make a ceremony of telling him so. That may help the doctor, but not the patient. When the patient is flirting with death, he may need someone who can help him get his things in order by helping him accept, and not reject, the passing acquaintance. When a child is facing death, the parents and the child can be helped in different ways. The child's questions can be answered honestly, but not excessively, and the parents can be kept fully informed and emotionally supported so that they can do the best possible job as parents of supporting a dying child. These are very difficult assignments. Physicians trained to hate death, conditioned to fear and shun death, are often ill prepared to fulfill the roles demanded of them. The real failure by doctors, in my experience, comes so often from failing to understand death, from failing themselves to have a philosophy that encompasses death and from having to work through their own guilt and shame and sense of failure at the time of death, that we do badly when we are most needed in this context.

I think I see this reality expressed in another way. Death, itself, is very poorly understood. As a pathologist, I am often asked what was the cause of death. The answer given is so often really improper and incorrect — pneumonia, coronary occlusion, etc., etc. But who in the world is studying the wonderful question of what is death. Who can give us scientific answers to this important inquiry. Really no one. We study conception, fertilization, gestation, delivery, illnesses of all kinds, all breeds of physiology, but it is a rare and uncommon person who is studying death scientifically. Thus we are destined to remain and will remain miserably ignorant of this important aspect of all of our lives. Why is no one studying death? We are afraid, inadequate and ill prepared by our culture, our families and our specific schooling.

DR. STACEY DAY: Thank you very much. I am going to go to the next question. I am going to ask Loanne *"Who is the closest to the dying patient, do you think? The Clergyman? Psychiatrist? Physician? or Friend? What do you think?"*

REGENT THRANE: I don't know if there is an overall answer. I suppose it depends on the individual. I can sense a very unique relationship between the doctor and the patient (I am thinking of the chronically ill patient). Maybe my role as

41

a woman makes me feel that certainly the family plays a very important part here. One would think of the clergy certainly - your pastor, your priest, play a very important role in guiding you through this particular time, but I don't know if you can pinpoint any one of these particular individuals as being the one who would be closest to an individual at the time of death.

DR. STACEY DAY: Thank you. Chaplain Neil, how would you face that question?

CHAPLAIN NEIL HERING: I am prejudiced. I hope the clergyman can be a friend and I hope the psychiatrist and the doctor can be a friend. My role as a pastor is to develop a friendship with a person who is dying. A part of me dies with the patient. Unless this is so, I don't think any of us are going to be very effective and we are really going to lose sight of what people go through.

DR. STACEY DAY: Thank you Neil. John Brantner, I am going to swing this question over to you. *"Is desertion and isolation more feared than death?"*

DR. JOHN BRANTNER: Oh sure, sure; and certainly more terrible and dangerous. The questions have been tending, the last few questions, to focus upon this matter of relationships at the time of dying. Again as with any horrible time, the presence of other people, not only physicians, psychiatrists, children, social workers, family, chaplain, but, *anybody, anybody,* nurse, housekeeper, the casual passerby — pain, or terror; everything is intensified by isolation and relieved by sharing. This is one thing I was going to

say in the matter of the conspiracy of silence. There is a dynamic that happens here. As with any of these things - I am sure especially for the dying patient, the dying person, and certainly with news of this sort, with pain, with distress, with sorrow - if we are going to be human we must share it. Partly, (this is Florida Scott Maxwell's idea) to learn about it ourselves, and partly to relieve ourselves of some of it. But as she pointed out, there comes a time when we must take it back to ourselves again. When we must take it back in, and when they approach us and say "How are you feeling today, dear?", we must answer "Quite well thank you." I would not class that as a conspiracy of silence. I would say one has to be sensitive in working, or relating to a dying person, as to where in this particular dynamic a person is. Does he now need to share this distress, to give us some of his burden, to learn about it through sharing it with us? Or is he at the point where he would just as soon not talk about the subject? Certainly we get tired of telling it over and over. There comes a time when we are ready to take it back and it may be that this is sometimes seen as a conspiracy of silence.

DR. STACEY DAY: Ignacio, would you say this thinking applies to the cancer patient?

DR. IGNACIO FORTUNY: I certainly think so. I don't think that the matter of dying is any different for any human being, regardless of the cause, particularly, I think if you have any degree of time, whether it is counted in days, weeks, months or years. The only thing that I really don't know how to interpret, as far as the act of death, would be in the rather sudden death of someone that is perfectly healthy. But, I think you would say, I would certainly think, that it is the same mechanisms. One of the things I would like to stress again with Dr. Brantner, is the conspiracy of silence, tying it in with what Dr. Good said, which results from the inadequacy of the individual caring for the patient, namely the doctors and nurses; they too fail. We don't like to see failure. Therefore, if we haven't got the courage to face the reality of this person's life and answer the question, when the question is posed to us "are we going to live?" we fumble by answering with very objective and scientific terms, something we really don't know. That's how the conspiracy begins, because then the doctor or the nurse gets caught in the game of trying to give an answer to something he or she doesn't know and the patient doesn't get any help at all, just the fumbling of words regarding his body. I think the conspiracy of silence, then, is a very real thing that never happens when, whoever is responsible, shares with the patient the reality of his state - whether it is immediate or distant death. Once the truth has been told to the person, and once the doctor has opened the gates for the settling of his own affairs, most of the emotional and behavioral inadequacies remove the basis for the conspiracy. How many of us go out in the sunshine every day after a few weeks of winter, when there is no sunshine, and look at the sun all day long, because it may not be there tomorrow. You can do just so much of that and then it hurts more than what you are trying to relieve. So it is with facing the reality of your own dying, you can put it aside only when it has been looked at and defined honestly; then acceptance follows.

DR. STACEY DAY: Thank you very much. I am going to give Bob Slater a new question. *"Can we prepare for sudden acute death arising from accidents or some unforeseeable circumstances? For example this is a nation on wheels and calculations tell us to expect 600-700 deaths for example, on a Thanksgiving Day, but no one knows who will be affected. Death in shock, death on roads. Would you anticipate death?"*

PROFESSOR ROBERT SLATER: I would like to approach it in two ways. There is a group that call themselves Equinox, surrounding the Harvard campus and medical center, who are doing some work in this regard with a health care team. That is, before the patient dies they have a funeral director, who is there in the group therapy sessions, to answer questions that this patient might have about his death. What happens? when does it happen? I think this is one way where we might follow very carefully a study where they are looking at preparation for death. I would assume the chaplain would have something to say on preparation for death and I think most of us believe this to be a function of religion. But I think the other thing our culture prepares us for is the kind of death that you are talking about in this way. Death is taboo. Death is practically contagious in our society and it is looked upon as unclean, unless you die a hero's death. It is one thing to die from some wasting disease, but, it is another thing to be killed going down the highway 80 miles an hour. Our culture seems to approve of death in one instance and to look upon it with much suspicion in another instance. Preparation for death has been with us a long time in all writings, in mythology for instance, yet, we seem to do an awfully good job of flunking the exam in preparing for it.

DR. STACEY DAY: Loanne, what would a woman's point of view possibly be?

REGENT THRANE: Thank you. I guess it is a case of you imagining it is going to happen to the other fellow. I can't imagine going out, or driving home on a Thanksgiving weekend, to have Thanksgiving dinner with Grandma, and think that you are going to be one of those statistics. I can't comprehend it. I am not sure that I personally am ready to, or do I really want to think that negatively. I perceive it as a negative point of view in this regard. I think this is an area that affects many of us and one for which we can't prepare as we do, certainly, with a long illness. I am not sure of what the answer is. I think it is a genuine concern, certainly something that has crossed my mind when you have a close scrape and you are sitting there saying "Thank God the car didn't veer to the left, but went to the right."

You have the blowout when there are no other cars on the road and you sort of sit there, shake and say: "There but for the grace of God I would have been". It is a concern certainly. I don't know how to deal with it and I guess I deal with it by ignoring it.

DR. STACEY DAY: That is very good because collectively we are all dealing with it by raising the question and I think we are doing some good. Dick Simmons go ahead if you will.

DR. RICHARD SIMMONS: I think the question is, should we prepare ourselves for sudden unexpected death so that it won't be unexpected? Yes. I think we should be prepared, but not for the reason given, although I think it is justified. I think we should be prepared in order to prevent it. I tell my wife, "By God you buckle that seatbelt because if you think you are going to get through this winter without another accident, you are mistaken." I think that represents a very important public health attitude. If we did use our seatbelts, we really would cut down on car accidents. In the same vein, we get vaccinated, or don't drink the dirty water, or don't visit India, or don't drink the water in Mexico. We are trying to avoid sudden death; and in that sense, I do feel you can prevent death through preparing for it.

DR. STACEY DAY: That is very good. John Brantner I think you will have something to say on that question.

DR. JOHN BRANTNER: I would simply

underline what Dr. Simmons has said. If we regard death of this sort as unthinkable, of course we will do nothing about it. If we regard it as unacceptable and think about it, then of course the next step is "what can we do about it?" We are careful in our personal lives, deciding not to drive after we have had an amount of whiskey, deciding to buckle seat belts, this kind of thing, deciding to grasp the stair railing as we go down the stairs, deciding to watch. [That one I did. From now on in Minnesota I will walk as though there was ice from October until March (ed. note: Dr. Brantner had earlier that week broken his arm falling on some stairs). I can see me going around with little tiny mincing steps from now on!] Then if we think about them, we can decide that certain deaths are unacceptable and this is a concept we can have and then, of course, the next step is what can we do about it. What can we do if they are unacceptable. If they are by and large preventable or reducible, what can we do? Only by taking thought will we take political and other action.

DR. STACEY DAY: Chaplain Hering, I am sure you are often called actually to such a thing like that in the hospital. Acute death in an accident. What would you say?

CHAPLAIN HERING: Just by adding that you have changed completely what I was going to say.

DR. STACEY DAY: I am sorry.

CHAPLAIN HERING: I guess instead of preparing for an acute sudden unexpected death, I see it as more important that we prepare ourselves in terms of seeing death and dying as a whole process that is going on around us and is part of reality. If I can work on this perspective, I think I can deal with it. Maybe that is the way I can deal with unexpected accidents that kill someone. This morning a group of us were talking about loss of control and to me death is the epitome of a loss of control. That is part of my experience in dying. If I can be human enough to realize that this is a dimension and an inherent ingredient of me as a person, I can help to live with that as part of me. Our Christian faith is there to help me realize that this is part of my humanity and that I am loved as that kind of person. We need to help each other start appreciating this dying part of us that goes on continuously.

DR. STACEY DAY: Thank you. Bob?

DR. ROBERT GOOD: Well I think that there is only one way to prepare for sudden and unexpected death and that is through our cultural heritage. Our poets constantly think on death, they constantly help us to face the possibilities of death, heroic death, death of soul, death of spirit. I really don't think that it is very active living or very exciting living, constantly to be avoiding death in a way that some have suggested. Look at all you youngsters going out there and skiing. The charm of skiing is that you are constantly seeking to be as close to death as possible and still being able to avoid it! If skiing isn't enough, you

45

take up sky diving, snowmobiling, etc. I think that being close to death and yet avoiding it is an exhilarating part of living. We know that the real way to avoid death on the highway is not to over crowd the highway. Seat belts are really an inconsequential, although temporarily slightly effective preventive measure. But they are not the real business. It is those overcrowded highways and the *chance* of accidents. How many would vote to reduce the traffic? We may, in our scholarly pursuit, have to be prepared to deal with the potentiality in our way of living of sudden death. But man is certainly Nature's most adaptable creature and there are veritable cultures as, for example, the eskimo's, perhaps unfortunately slipping away, but a very exciting culture whose major cultural adaptation is represented by constant exposure to death. I would answer this question by saying that there is only one preparation, one way of preparing for the eventuality of unexpected sudden death and that is to do as I think Dr. Brantner recommended last week, "think on death whenever we get a chance, try to think and plan for it daily." I have been practicing all this last week. I have been thinking about death when I shave. It's caused me a few times to come close to cutting my throat, but I am getting practice in thinking about death - my own, not someone else's.

DR. STACEY DAY: *"Should household members be deprived of all pleasurable activities following or preceding death of a family member?"* Ignacio?

DR. IGNACIO FORTUNY: Having come from the Latin culture, where death and birth are two parts of every day living, (because birth doesn't necessarily take place in the hospital but may take place next door in the home - and the same thing with death) I can't divorce myself from at least 35 years of influence in my life regarding the involvement of family and dear ones in the process of being born and dying. In relationship to this, I think my philosophy as to my own preparation for death, is separated, in my own mind, into two practical aspects. Death to me is being without me and I can't conceive that, so, there is nothing I can do about death itself. I can't handle that until the day I die. As far as the process of dying itself - I think that is what concerns me. I only know and understand the slow process of dying. Sudden death I do not understand. I like to conceive of my dying as something rather placid, not only in the sense of bodily discomforts, or pain, but also in the sense of emotional peace by gathering my meaningful relationships about me so that we can really hold hands and be helped in a very selfish manner by using them, as much as I can. Since I know I fear loneliness, it is perhaps one of the worst things that a human being can be subjected to. So I would say in answer to the question, I would not think that it is a good practice to separate loved ones before or after death or from allowing them to express their true spontaneous feelings about their loss. This is because it is very real to them and I think death, whether we live next door or whether we live a 100 miles away from each other, is a family event. Many writers on the subject have mentioned there are 4 or 5 steps in the final acceptance of the process of dying and final death, and I think that the loved ones lag at least two steps behind the dying person.

DR. STACEY DAY: Thank you. Bob Slater?

PROFESSOR ROBERT SLATER: I appreciate very much Dr. Fortuny's last statement because if you will take Kubler Ross's steps of procedures in death and dying, follow them from the discipline of funeral service, you will see the family go through the identical steps, but as the good doctor says, 2 or 3 behind the patient. I appreciate his personal reference. We used to have this in this country - the multigenerational home where grandparents and parents and often times cousins, aunts and uncles lived together - death was common and when somebody died they knew exactly what had happened. In our single generational homes today, with the great big garage and the small living space, we tend to say that if we are going to do something important, we are going to go away from home to do it. And we go away to be born and we go away to die. I think if we bring that back into the context, it will help people return as quickly as they can to normal living. You don't do this by convincing them that nothing has happened. You don't do it by hiding what has happened. You face it. You face it head on. You react to it and you then draw from others the strength to return to the normal mainstream of life. This is one thing that is happening within the churches. The Catholic Church in their new funeral rite out of Vatican II, has really reversed almost the whole procedure. This is something that we like very much because we are seeing so many changing funeral ceremonies - no longer sterile rigid procedures, but, instead flexible and adaptable to the people that are in grief. You are working through their grief, not something that somebody said in a book or a ritual should be done. In these ceremonies, the family can get together and dissipate among many people, the strong feeling each one can accept more quickly their own and return to the mainstream of life.

DR. STACEY DAY: Before I leave the question I think we should get a woman's point of view. Loanne?

REGENT THRANE: Could I ask you to restate the question?

DR. STACEY DAY: Yes. *"Should household members be deprived of all pleasurable activities following or preceding the death of a family member?"*

REGENT THRANE: Oh certainly not! I think that the family does react. I concur with the last speaker. I think that we want to encourage them to show their grief, to feel their grief. It is a stage that they have to go through. To suggest that they must isolate themselves, I think, is unrealistic and really unhealthy.

DR. STACEY DAY: Thank you very much.

PROFESSOR ROBERT SLATER: May I add one thing that I think those of you have been in these experiences will bear out. 9 out of 10 times, when I am in a funeral situation with bereaved families, before the afternoon or evening is over somebody will make the statement that we ought to do this more often.

DR. STACEY DAY: John Brantner?

DR. IGNACIO FORTUNY: May I say something Stacey? I think the idea of the old fashioned wake is very important because this is exactly what the family was allowed to do. They were allowed to cry together, even to the point of hysteria, without being criticised for not accepting the fact that their loved one was dead. And it was a perfectly acceptable social event that started out as an uncontrolled emotion from grief - crying, and toward the earlier hours of the morning, whiskey took over and tranquilized the emotional agitation of the grieving person.

DR. STACEY DAY: I think I could add a rider to that. People in the East, particularly in India, where death and birth are very much family occasions, underline what you have just said Ignacio. Family relationships are extremely important in the East. John Brantner, *"Will the husband feel resentment toward the terminally ill wife? Does he react as a child would to a mother's desertion?"*

DR. JOHN BRANTNER: I will answer it much more generally. Some husbands may. Some husbands perhaps should. The question reflects an interest in the mixed feelings that we all experience at a death, at a terminal separation in the relationship. We have always left things undone, we have always come to the termination of death feeling that we would have done differently had we but known. One of the areas in which as a society, as a people, we need instruction, we need help, is in awareness of the facts of grief. What are the things that happen? To know that it is perfectly normal to have your sorrow mixed with anger - To have your sorrow mixed with relief that the person has finally died - To entertain at this time, as we do always of course, unworthy feelings as well as worthy ones, and some frightening ones as well - To know that these are normal, that we don't require the services of a psychiatrist or a psychologist because we do these unusual things in grief. I think this is the thing the question is reflecting. We should have sources of support in these times, and certainly the understanding that we will experience this kind of frightening mixed feeling, that this is part of grief.

DR. STACEY DAY: Thank you John. Dick Simmons, *"Do family members and relatives often feel they should be blamed for a patient's death?"*

DR. RICHARD SIMMONS: Families commonly feel that they are to blame for a relative's death. Transplant surgeons are often viewed as vultures and in a sense that is true. We hang around the Neurosurgeons until one of their patients dies and then we try to get the organs. In a sense, the family feels guilt

48

about this death. In every one of those sudden deaths of young people whose organs are usable, they *do* feel enormous amounts of guilt. Somewhere along the line they didn't watch their child who drowned in the pool, or they let him out on the street, or there was some event which led up to the death which, if they had taken a different route, the patient wouldn't have gone there and wouldn't have died suddenly. On the other hand, maybe they argued that morning, and there is a lot of guilt in all our relationships; they may have had some undesirable thoughts such as "My God why doesn't he go away and go back to school" or whatever. I think this guilt surrounds most deaths and I think it's fairly clear. We have noted on a few occasions that the memorial of the gift of the organ (I am not trying to advertise), represents something very meaningful to the family of the patient who dies, as expiation in part of their guilt.

DR. STACEY DAY: Thank you very much. Bob Good. This is a very broad one. "*Is there a tendency to maintain a front of cheerfulness in the family which breaks down later on when the moment of death approaches?*" And death has taken place subsequently?

DR. ROBERT GOOD: Well certainly when we are dealing with chronic illness and illness where there may possibly be a way out, the family will whistle in the dark a great deal. I think that we see this constantly and they will become overly enthusiastic, over zealous of the potential of modern medical biology and therapeutics. I think that we see this often. On the other hand, we see often just the opposite side of the coin. We see a giving up too early on the part of some family members. I think these are extremely complicated things. I think family and relatives, no matter how close they are, experience all of the human emotions in dealing with the death process. It is not only guilt, but hostility, joy, relief that it is not them, even genuine sadness, all of these things are part of the mixture of emotions expressed by people dealing with something that is inevitable, something they don't like to deal with and sometimes that seems offensive to them.

DR. STACEY DAY: Thank you. Perhaps you have overlapped to some degree a question I am going to ask Chaplain Hering. "*Are relatives often guilt ridden because of angry wishes toward the dead person?*" And then there is a rider to the question. "*Can they themselves become sick?*" I will generalize. I am not asking you for a physician's point of view, but as a non-physician. Generalize sick, not as a specific illness, but shall we say their attitudes are "not healthy?"

CHAPLAIN NEIL HERING: Situations like this happen with the relatives when they see what their loved one has gone through after a long suffering, especially with Leukemia. The families will sometimes say to me; "I found myself wishing that my husband or wife would die" and then in the next breath they will say; "But I shouldn't think that way." You can pick up, right away, the guilt that is behind that kind of a wish. There is a lot of that and I think it is heightened by the kind of medical care we're capable of giving, because we can deal with so many more traumatic illnesses. However, it takes such traumatic medications and drugs to treat them. Because all this can take a long period of time, these kinds of feelings in the family are only heightened and intensified, especially when they know there will be only a temporary remission and not a cure. In answer to the rider: Where guilt over feelings like "I wish my loved one would die", is present regardless of it being expressed out of anger or love, this has a way of making that person real sick inside - that tears their guts apart. Eventually, if they are not able to share it with someone, or talk it out, or look at it as being normal, and as a natural human reaction, it is also going to get them physically ill.

DR. STACEY DAY: Thank you. John?

DR. JOHN BRANTNER: The studies that have been done, not looking at feelings of guilt or anger after death, but simply looking at survival after death, have corroborated what we have known from the beginning. Sir Thomas Morton's tombstone says: (he is buried in the same grave with his wife) "She first deceased, he for a little tried to live without her, liked it not and died." This is a common reaction, the death of a spouse within a year of the other spouse. There have been now two major studies that show that death rates, mortality from all causes, goes up by a factor of 5. 5 times as many deaths among relatives in the year following a significant death. Not only can people become sick in a generalized sense, they can become mortally sick following a significant death. This has been clearly established, the rates are different. If it is unexpected, accidental traumatic death of a wife during the middle years, the death rates of surviving husbands go up by a factor of 40 in the 12 months following.

DR. STACEY DAY: I am going to give this question specifically and only to Bob Slater. *"What purpose do funerals fulfill?"*

PROFESSOR ROBERT SLATER: It seems to me that if we look upon a funeral for the intention for which it is given in most cultures, and they tell us they haven't found a culture yet that has not had some sort of a ceremony or funeral rite, and if we refer back to the good doctor, we emphasize again that it gives an approval to the feelings and the emotions that people have at the time of a separation crisis, in this instance, death. All of our functions, where we express strong emotions, have had established around them rites and ceremonies. It helps many people act through or to say things that they can not ordinarily express on their own or without the help of a liturgy or a rite. I think there is something further that is important in this culture. We talk a lot about death and the dead and the relationships that go with it. It seems to me the real importance of a funeral has to be as much a testimony to the fact that a life has been lived as much as it has to the fact that a death has occured. The death is an empirical fact. The life that has touched many people, whether they were important or unimportant, is very important to that family circle however large it might be. It seems to me that they have the right to work through their feelings the way they want to work them through and with expressions that are meaningful to them and not by that which might be decreed by some authority. The ability to work through these strong feelings, that to me is in our culture in this current time, is the purpose of the funeral and I think history will prove it has been the same throughout the ages.

DR. STACEY DAY: Thank you very much. We have only 5 minutes left. I am going to give the panel somewhat less than a minute each for this question. *"If a patient expresses a wish to die at home, do you feel this wish should be honored? Even if it brings death sooner than if in the hospital? Or if death could have been avoided entirely with hospital treatment?"* Bob Good.

DR. ROBERT GOOD: I think you must take the particular individual circumstances and deal with those. It is difficult to generalize on this point. Speaking to that question directly, I can conceive of times when it is better to make possible an easy and pleasant death of the patient surrounded by family at home. That today should be and will be an exception but not a rare exception. I think that under other circumstances, the conditions, comfort and supportive care and the possibility of effective therapeutics, is only available in the hospital, therefore, it is better to urge strongly that the family seek really professional therapeutic care in the hospital.

DR. STACEY DAY: Dick Simmons, how would you answer that?

DR. RICHARD SIMMONS: In general, I think the answer is yes. The patient should be able to go wherever he wants. The physician must make sure he understands the consequences of his action and the alternatives to it. On the other hand, I do think that one shouldn't make a sentimental attachment to dying at home, although I feel that perhaps this panel and the audience do have such a feeling. There are really good functional reasons why hospitals were set up to avoid, particularly in a highly specialized society, fragmenting the patient who is dying at home. A dying patient would require the rest of the family to stay at home and take care of him; which is not a very functional thing to do in our society. I think there are real functions that the hospital can serve, although perhaps we do need an improvement there.

DR. STACEY DAY: Thank you. Loanne?

REGENT THRANE: I guess I am amazed at the question. The thought of dying at home or being given the option, particularly where there is a possibility that some help might be available to prolong life or indeed for cure, just is unacceptable. Possibly the age I grew up in, the environment in which I grew up, I

51

can see a person, myself if you will, dying in a hospital. This seems more familiar more comfortable to me as an individual.

DR. STACEY DAY: I think that is a very interesting point because it shows the direction in which our cultural attitudes are moving. Ignacio?

DR. IGNACIO FORTUNY: I think again when we talk about death in this society, when people talk about dying at home, they don't necessarily mean the house which means home to them, but the town or an area close to their friends and relatives and endearing human beings that they lived and toiled with. I think that is what I interpret in the question, "Can I go home and die?" rather than the actual death at home and I think they have the right to. I think the question is too black and white because it is very difficult at times to know what particular treatment may save the life of the person, if you are talking about dying in the sense that I interpret it. I don't think the question of keeping the patient in the hospital will give him life everlasting, but by making an issue of the fact that the net result is an unhappy patient and a family which after death may regret not allowing their loved one that wish.

DR. STACEY DAY: Chaplain Hering?

CHAPLAIN NEIL HERING: I see a lot of subtle pressures within the hospital on patients and their families that make it very difficult for them to make a decision on whether to stay, or go home and die. I am 100% behind the patient for the right to make a choice, as long as they know the consequences. But, there are things that make them feel quite guilty as if they were going up against a big establishment that doesn't want them to give up and die, but wants them to fight for life at all costs. This makes it very difficult for a patient under this kind of indirect pressure to make a choice, but I think they really should be able to.

DR. STACEY DAY: Thank you. John Brantner?

DR. JOHN BRANTNER: I think the question would not be so difficult if we strengthen the tendency that we are already seeing now: not so much the choice between bringing the patient home to his family to die, as the possibility of inserting the family, involving the family more in the hospital: of making being in the hospital less of a significant separation from family and from community: of changing visitation, of changing the involvement of the family in the patient's care: of moving not so much in the direction of sending people home with all of the therapeutic appliances, as rather bringing the home to the hospital.

DR. STACEY DAY: Bob Slater what would you say?

PROFESSOR ROBERT SLATER: There is a saying, and I think the two previous speakers have said this, "Home is where the heart is" and I would agree so much with John that I think I would prefer to die in the hospital, particularly if I could have my family and those I love with me when I needed their strength and support in the process.

DR. STACEY DAY: Before I close the panel could I end on a somewhat poetic note. We actually needed a Humanitarian here or somebody from the Humanities. I don't mean the panel is not humanitarian! But it appears to me we have been discussing death and there has been little emphasis on life. In a personal sense, I don't know if peace has any meaning without antecedent war. Does death have any meaning without life? Since we are talking about death and life, this engraving may be familiar to some of you. It is in St. Paul's Church in Baltimore and it is dated 1692. It relates to a way of living and perhaps I can adjourn with this Desiderata for life:

"Go placidly amid the noise and haste and remember what peace there may be in silence. As far as possible without surrender be on good terms with all persons. Speak your truth quietly and clearly; and listen to others, even the dull and ignorant; they too have their story. Avoid loud and aggressive persons, they are vexations to the spirit. If you compare yourself with others, you may become vain and bitter; for always there will be greater and lesser persons than yourself. Enjoy your achievements as well as your plans. Keep interested in your own career, however humble; it is a real possession in the changing fortunes of time. Exercise caution in your business affairs for the world is full of trickery. But let this not blind you to what virtue there is; many persons strive for high ideals, and everywhere life is full of heroism. Be yourself. Especially, do not feign affection. Neither be cynical about love; for in the face of all aridity and disenchantment it is perennial as the grass. Take kindly the counsel of the years, gracefully surrendering the things of youth. Nurture strength of spirit to shield you in sudden misfortune. But do not distress yourself with imaginings. Many fears are born of fatigue and loneliness. Beyond a wholesome discipline, be gentle with yourself. You are a child of the universe, no less than the trees and the stars; you have a right to be here. And whether or not it is clear to you, no doubt the universe is unfolding as it should. Therefore be at peace with God, whatever you conceive him to be, and whatever your labors and aspirations, in the noisy confusion of life keep peace with your soul. With all its sham, drudgery and broken dreams, it is still a beautiful world. Be careful. Strive to be happy".

Death—The Child Patient and The Physician

DR. STACEY DAY: Today we are going to focus on matters dealing with death and the child. We are happy to have with us Father D. Edward Mathie, Rector of the Jesuit College, St. Paul. Dr. George Williams, Associate Professor of Psychiatry and Public Health is joining us for the first time, as also are Dr. Mark Nesbit, Associate Professor of Pediatrics, and Florence Kahn, a pediatric Nurse Clinician. We renew companionship with Professor Mulford Sibley and Professor John Brantner and greet as a new member of our panel Dr. Jasper Hopkins, Assoicate Professor in the University faculty of Philosophy.

You are all very welcome, so without further ado we will get the program under way. You will remember that our goal has been not to try to teach, but to develop these meetings as seminars for mutual growth. It is a two way street. You as a student body have raised the questions and I regard the panel as a sounding board for your thoughts. Together we can interrelate on these important issues, and perhaps out of the entire program will come ideas and thought processes that will help all of us to reach personal understanding of how we as individuals will decide to react to the questions raised. I feel it important to stress that I regard, as equally important, that your input, your questions, and the practical and theoretical levels of discussion they raise, are *no less important to the panel*, for by this interaction the panelists themselves are enabled to grow and to develop new directions for their substantive disciplines. As on previous occasions, I will present first the same question to all members of the panel and then go on from there. The first question reads: *"Do you feel there is a particular age at which children are best equipped to deal with the facts of death?"* Mark Nesbit?

DR. MARK NESBIT: Well no. I don't think there is. I think there is a period of time, when children don't have any understanding of what death is and never do, so, therefore, don't respond to death like adults or teenagers. I would say up to the age of about 5 or 6 the child, per se, has no understanding of what we consider to be death. Death means a separation to them from their home or from their family, and they feel safe as long as they aren't going to be separated from their family or have some sort of understanding with their parents that they are not going to be left alone. I don't think that they react in any respect like the older child or the adult, so in that case I think they are considerably different. Of course infants up to 5 or 6 have probably never even heard the word death. They have no understanding of death even if they do hear the word, and you could tell the child that he was going to die every day and it would mean nothing to him. If you told him that he was no longer going to see his mother and father only then would he react in an anxious way. I think that as far as children are concerned the most difficult to understand are probably the teenage girls. My experience has been that these girls are the most reluctant to deal with death.

DR. STACEY DAY: Thank you Mark. I am going to give this question next to Ed Mathie.

FATHER ED MATHIE: I would think that my experience is very limited on that Stacey. The only thing that I could say would be the obvious; that I think children vary in the depth of their experience and I would think that from different ages they would be able to react just differently, depending upon what has happened within their own family. I would guess possibly even if they have experienced the loss of a dog or something that has been very close to them, that might help them come to some understanding of death.

DR. STACEY DAY: Thank you Ed. As a matter of fact that is a very good point because the next question is on the death of a loved animal or pet so we will come back to this, but I thank you for raising the issue. Florence Kahn, how would you answer the first question.

NURSE FLORENCE KAHN: I would agree with what Dr. Nesbit said. Many times the younger child, say from 4 to 9, has a lot of fantasies about things - many wild ideas. Often he will play games in mimic of the adult world around him. But when he plays Cowboys and Indians he shoots you dead and then he gets right up again . . . that is generally what his understanding of death is until the age of 9. At that age children really begin to get some comprehension of the permanence of death. The nurses on the station are often concerned with the understanding of a child when he asks "Am I going to die?" For most young children 4-9, the nurses assume he is not asking the big question. It is better to ask him if he is feeling poorly that day, or respond to the fact that he is lonesome for his mother. It is the teenager nurses are often concerned about and I hope it will be discussed later on. The major concern is that in terms of comprehension and general coping strengths, is it good or bad to share the knowledge of a prognosis with a teenager?

DR. STACEY DAY: Thank you very much. Mulford Sibley.

PROFESSOR MULFORD SIBLEY: Well if you agree with Wordsworth that heaven lies about us in our infancy, then it seems to me the child comes from heaven in a sense and then the prison house begins to close in on him. In heaven you can hardly conceive of what death means. It is only later on in the development of the child, I think, that he has, or he begins to have an awareness, as has been said here, of death and sex. These are in a sense discovered at about the same time. I mean they become problems. I would just add one other sentence. It does seem to me it is never too early for a child to observe death - how he perceives it will differ radically from the period of infancy to, let's say, the period of adolescence.

DR. STACEY DAY: Thank you. Jasper Hopkins. Do you have some thoughts on that question?

PROFESSOR JASPER HOPKINS: Well there are a number of senses of "understand",

I guess, when you ask the question of when can the child best understand. In one sense he can best understand (or at least he is most ready to find out something) about death when he asks the question. Children are very inquisitive - they discover from television or sometimes from Sunday school or sometimes from playmates, something about death, and they ask their parents. That is the time when one should try to answer these questions. The other sense of understanding, which involves experiencing some emotions and appreciating the phenomenon of death and feeling its trauma, would of course come much later. And I agree here with the clinicians that the child won't be able to understand at an early age. Maybe I could also ask a question of you - what counts as a child? Are we counting teenagers as children?

DR. STACEY DAY: I have my own ideas, but since I am the moderator and Mark Nesbit is a pediatrician, let's get an authoritative definition.

DR. MARK NESBIT: Well it really is an administrative thing because they tell us that I can't admit a patient after he is 15 and 11/12ths. Now with some patients I cheat - that is if the patient is going to do well! But if the patient doesn't look as if he is going to do very well, then I go the other way.

DR. STACEY DAY: Yes I think for the purpose of this panel, and as I believe, I think 15. For the purpose of this panel let's say 15 is the cutoff age. Thank you.

Now let me come to the two psychiatrists or people interested in the area of psychology and psychiatry. George Williams would you answer that question?

DR. GEORGE WILLIAMS: Yes I think I would agree with what has been said by other people and I think that this is a concept that is so difficult for a child to understand that they have to build, immediately build, defenses against it. If they have experienced the loss of a loved one, a family member, a close friend, and equally in importance a pet, then they are faced with the problem of trying to answer this big question of what is death? It is so upsetting that we see children, and I will identify the 5 to 6 year old age group and younger, going through a considerable amount of wasting of time, energy and effort, and pain, sometimes because parents don't attempt to meet their questions honestly and directly. But even if they are, then the youngster has to go through the counter phobic phenomena, playing dead as Florence just pointed out to us, proving to themselves and to the world that they really aren't afraid of it. In youngsters of this age with whom I have had the privilege and pleasure of working, it seems to be that they don't really understand death. Maybe the 9-year-old does, and maybe above that, but at about 5 or 6, I think they get the idea this is a game. For I think that when we talk of death in certain ways to a child we can frighten them. For it is in my opinion, impossible for the finite mind to think

of itself as not existing. And so perhaps we too join them in their games.

DR. STACEY DAY: Thank you. John Brantner.

DR. JOHN BRANTNER: The world of the child is of course, to me, a relatively closed one and a very mysterious one, and one of the most mysterious aspects of that world is the one that has been alluded to here; the fact that children experience things without understanding them. The child does experience death. The child knows death as has been said and as will be said in the next question, in creatures that he runs up against. He experiences it sometimes in the death of his grandparents, his parents, occasionally siblings, although this is rare now. The child experiences perhaps without full adult understanding. If, in our own distress, we use the excuse that the child doesn't understand and therefore will not work it through with the child, there can be horrible consequences. For example, children who are convinced that they are responsible for the death of the grandparents. Children who believe that because they were naughty or because they did something specific, the grandparent has gone and will never come back. It is very important to realize that distinction. Children do not have perhaps an adult understanding of death, but they experience it, they know it, and they have their own developed fantasies about it. And I think that it is extraordinarily important, especially in the death of others,

58

that we respond to this need of the children. Responding to the child's need and not our own. When he says:

"She went to the Baker's to buy him some bread when she came back the poor dog was dead."

What does this mean? To respond not in terms of our own needs and our fears, but to try as best we can to respond in terms of the child's need. The same with sex. The kid who says "Where did I come from?" - was delivered a long embarassed sex education lecture, and at the end of it his father says; "Does that answer your question son," and the boy says, "Well no, not exactly, Jimmy next door said he came from Cincinnati and I wondered where I came from." (Laughter)

DR. STACEY DAY: Thank you John. To some degree the next two questions have been answered in part. The next question was; *"Many children's first exposure with death is the death of a loved animal. How do you help a child through this crisis and have him develop a healthy attitude toward death?"* Ed, how would you approach a child in that situation?

FATHER ED MATHIE: I think first of all that there have been reactions such as the one I have heard, where people say that the dog has gone to heaven. So I say that as a religious panel member: this is not an adequate answer. You know I would agree with John, I guess, that too how can we explain what the very real situation is? What has happened? What is it, what has caused the death? Now I think the one thing is that

with something like an animal there is some replacement for a loss. This is where I don't think you can replace say a grandmother or a parent or a close family member but I think a youngster's mind can become taken up again with some other animal or with some other pet. Now I wouldn't know whether this would be good or not good, but maybe the question would then be could they experience or learn more from a loss like this or not? I don't know. You know I am not trying to punish the child, I am just wondering is it a worthwhile question that we ask. Do we give them a pet right away or may the loss be very helpful and good for them for a period?

DR. STACEY DAY: Thank you Ed. I will ask the same question to Jasper Hopkins. How would you answer that?

PROFESSOR JASPER HOPKINS: Well I think the real danger here is to try to impose information upon a child. And I think, therefore, that you have to ask him how *he* responds to this, what questions he has. Does he want to bury the dog in the back yard? Then go out and bury the dog with him. Does he want to get another dog? You have to direct yourself to the question *he has,* and the main thing is to ask what is bothering *him.*

DR. STACEY DAY: Fine. Since some of the others have touched on that, I am going to ask the next question, I am going to start with John Brantner on this. *"How does a child view his own death? If he is healthy?"* I presume that means if he is in what we call normal good health.

"And secondly, if he is ill?" I would presume that would take a hospitalized child. *"How does a child view his own death?"*

DR. JOHN BRANTNER: Since I have not worked with children at all I would rather defer answering. I could only say that I suspect he at very best, does the same job we do. He views it as inconceivable.

DR. STACEY DAY: Thank you John. Florence Kahn, have you, as a pediatric nurse, anything to add to that?

NURSE FLORENCE KAHN: Looking at the healthy child, I think we have already discussed different age comprehensions of death. If you examine your own upbringing as far as understanding of death is concerned, our society and cultural family patterns aren't very helpful. If they shield you from it at all, how can you form any kind of ideas about it? However, if you have had pets and lost them, I think that is the way a growing child begins to gain his experiences as far as what he thinks about death. For the ill child, I guess the first thing I think about is his age and normal growth and development. Where a child is growth wise, at that time, is a bridge to his coping and thinking as an ill child. Often nurses will get hung up with their own personal questions and fears about death as individuals and impose them on a child. That is where the nursing staff has the most difficult time, because they haven't answered the questions themselves, let alone try and help a child. If you can remember what the normal growth and development needs are, and that a child wants to be with his parents, he wants to be comforted, he wants to know that we are going to make him better so he can get up and play - you will be far more helpful. The other thing I always remember is that if you treat a child like he is sick all the time, he is going to respond like a sick child and really sense that something is wrong. With parents, the common reaction will be that they become over protective and very over solicitous of the child because they have found out that something terrible is going to happen to him. But as nursing staff, if you can set limits, if you can play with the child and make his life in the hospital as normal as possible, then again he will cope *better* with his illness and have fewer fantasies about why everyone is so tense and serious.

DR. STACEY DAY: Thank you very much. Now I am going to give the next question to a pediatrician, Mark Nesbit. *"Do you feel a chronically ill child should be told of his approaching death?"*

DR. MARK NESBIT: First I would like to comment on the last question because I think that most children look at death through their parents and how their parents have responded to it in the past. They perceive exactly what the parents are going through, or the hospital personnel that are taking care of them if the parents aren't there. The children respond to how the people around them have reacted to the hospitalization. As far as the question concerning whether you tell a chronically ill child whether he is going to die, when I know the child is going to die soon, I attempt to make possible for the child to discuss with the parents and with the other people around, his or her concerns about death. I personally, at the time of diagnosis of an incurable disease, do not "spell it out". I do not hit them over the head with the fact that they are going to die. I do it in otherways. I sublimate it to some extent. But I do think that with a child, you will have a chance to discuss death. I make every attempt to allow such a chance of discussing actually what the child thinks about death. More important, I find out ways to help the child discuss with the parents what the parents think about death. For it turns out that death usually isn't sad to the child that actually dies, *it is to the people that are left behind.* That is who we have to be more concerned about. It is those who are left that have to be involved with anxieties of death, not the child who has died.

DR. STACEY DAY: George Williams.

DR. GEORGE WILLIAMS: I would just like to add this - I think we have to look at this very carefully in terms of the individual child with whom we are dealing. I think many times we transmit to the child that he is going to die. I submit that sometime when you are in the room and an entourage of doctors comes in to look at the patient, don't look at the patient, but look at the doctors' faces. See what kind of feeling and thought and impression you are picking up from them. It can be rather frightening. Those of us who work with the child later and we have cleared all the things that have been talked about in relation, find that they are really somewhat relieved to be dealt with directly and honestly, with integrity and with sensitivity, and I hope with a modicum of intelligence. It is at that time, then, that the tremendous burden is put upon us to share with them all we can to make the remainder of their life as productive and as pleasant as possible. Frequently, you know they will kind of catch you up. I had a youngster say to me a couple of years ago, when I was setting limits on some self destructive behavior and he was fourteen; "You know that is a hell of a way to treat a guy that is going to die." And I said; "And I would be a hell of a friend if I let you continue to do this kind of thing and sit here and watch you hurt yourself," And he said; "That's right, I am not causing my own death." And then he said; "will you be here when I die?" And I said; "you bet I'll be here," and was.

DR. STACEY DAY: Thank you very much. I am going to go into what I think will be an area that is not concrete. I want to give this question to Mulford Sibley and to Jasper Hopkins and then I'll throw it open to the panel if necessary. It is a rather long question, but see if you can field it. It is perhaps a nonmedical philosophical situation but it concers us all. Social conditions may in a sense determine both life and death. A child born in the ghetto, when in utero, because his mother may conceivably be poor and malnourished, may never be able to achieve the potential, underline the word potential, of a child born into a well provided home. Thus, I have heard a case argued that in the old days rickets and other diseases were especially a legacy of the poor. If this philosophy be true, illness and death in children of the poor is potentially great. Such children are born with the potential as it were of an early death. Comment.

PROFESSOR MULFORD SIBLEY: Well I think it is obviously true that they are. If you are born in the ghetto or some other deprived area, the chances of your dying prematurely are greater and it's a simple fact, it seems to me. But even here, going back to the previous question, I think in so far as you are dealing with the child, you shouldn't underestimate his intelligence in pointing out some of these facts. But the social side I think is pretty obvious.

DR. STACEY DAY: Jasper?

PROFESSOR JASPER HOPKINS: Yes I agree.

DR. STACEY DAY: Ed Mathie? Were you going to add anything to that?

FATHER ED MATHIE: No.

DR. STACEY DAY: Does any other member of the panel want to add anything or detract from this? They pass it up I guess. Let's go to one that is more general then. *"Should children be included in grief or sent away?"* John Brantner?

DR. JOHN BRANTNER: It should be clear what my answer to that will be. Yes of course it is very wrong to exclude the child from any of the occasions of family solidarity and family growth. It is very wrong to exclude children from situations of grief and loss. This is one of the errors that hospitals make in excluding children from visiting - children under the age 12 or the age of 14, or whatever, from visiting very, very sick and indeed dying patients, dying relatives. The child should not be excluded but indeed should be included. One of the things that I think should be changed socially in our country is the inclusion, the deliberate inclusion of children in funerals. I think that this would, for one thing, improve the funeral. I can conceive of no more significant statement than a child's crying out or laughing or playing at the occasion of burying one of our beloved dead. Also, I think that it would have a significant effect on the child in his growing in solidarity with the community and his family. I think our exclusion of the child in times of grief is very, very wrong. Again it is the groundwork for development of some very peculiar fantasies on the part of the child.

DR. STACEY DAY: Florence Kahn.

NURSE FLORENCE KAHN: I don't have much more to add to that except that very often when you pull a child from the family and bring him into the hospital, the siblings are left with guilty feelings. We had one situation where the mother related that she had been away from the other siblings and not paying any attention and when she finally asked her six or seven year old why he was so withdrawn and what was wrong he said; "well isn't it my fault that my brother is in the hospital?" So that even for a simple hospitalization you really have to include the other children in the why's and bring them to visit the hospitalized child.

DR. STACEY DAY: Thank you Florence. Ed Mathie?

FATHER ED MATHIE: I think here I learned, in being able to go in Milwaukee and being involved in the central city there for some time, which is one place that if we want to talk about people who have been deprived in many ways, they *haven't* been deprived in this area. Their children are all present at funerals and the childrens friends are present at the funeral. They all partake beautifully, I think, in a way where we exclude many times and say "oh don't ask their children to come - they shouldn't partake in this sorrow." And they really do, in a very beautiful way as John was saying. I have seen it and I wish that some of the other funerals that I have attended, the children had been there. I think they learn, participate and partake.

DR. STACEY DAY: Thank you Ed. Does any other member of the panel want to answer that question? Yes, go ahead Mark.

DR. MARK NESBIT: I would like to make a comment. When I deal with a child who has leukemia, which at the present time is an incurable disease, it is im-

portant how the parents decide to handle the rest of the children. What to tell them. I find that it is very much a clue of *that* families' situation as to how they have responded. I think it is a good situation, when a family discusses the problems with the other children very honestly. It is the parents who try to hide the problems, who talk at home behind closed doors where the other children, by listening at the door, don't here all the facts. Their fantasies rise and they become convinced that they are at fault. This is the situation that I see in 50% of the children from families who are associated with a dying child. It is not surprising this guilt appears for siblings have hit them (when parents are not watching), or stuck their tongues out at them in anger. Many of the siblings think that actually these incidents are the cause of why the child is in the hospital. If the child is very ill (going in and out of the hospital) often times siblings of the patient develop increasing guilt that they were involved. On the other hand, there is the situation where parents have forgotten entirely about the other children. All the input is directed to the ill child. The other children are left to take care of themselves but they are the ones that we are going to have to deal with after the sick child actually dies.

DR. STACEY DAY: Go ahead George.

DR. GEORGE WILLIAMS: I would like to add that I think this can be a real growth experience for the whole family, to be able to grieve together. It is in this process of grieving that many of these very destructive and interpunitive fantasies come out in a sort of almost open confessional kind of thing and guilt can well, very well be relieved. I think the family that can really grieve together, then, can gain mutual support and go on from there and actually become much closer. The other thing that occurred to me is the fact that very frequently when a death occurs in a family, well intentioned and well meaning adults will focus their attention upon the parents who have lost the child and there is relatively little attention paid to the youngsters in the family. Now this is defended against by saying: "Well they are too little to understand, they won't know, they won't remember," but actually working with these youngsters is awfully important and I think one of the reasons which accounts for our not doing it, is the fact that this is really an extremely painful thing for us, as adults, to do at times.

DR. STACEY DAY: Thank you very much. Mulford, why don't you have a go at this question. I think it could be generalized even for non-medical men because grief affects us all. Should children be included in grief? or sent away? How would you look at it?

PROFESSOR MULFORD SIBLEY: Well I think I would agree with everything that has been said here. I think they ought to be included. Just as you include them in other family ceremonies and so on. They ought to be part of the family and no matter how young they are, as far as I'm concerned.

DR. STACEY DAY: And just to round out everybody's opinion of that, Jasper, why don't you come in and say something?

PROFESSOR JASPER HOPKINS: Well I think this is right. But I think also that, on the other side, one should remember that many children, especially the ones who do not identify with death, are not able to understand completely; and it would be very strange to drag them along to something they are not really interested in. I remember when my brother was in an iron lung with polio. It wasn't open to me to go to the hospital to see him, but, indeed I had no desire to do so.

DR. STACEY DAY: Do you think that *this* generation might have a desire to go?

PROFESSOR JASPER HOPKINS: Well it is sort of a Doctor Welby generation. They might like to see some of the excitement.

DR. STACEY DAY: Thank you. Go ahead Mark.

DR. MARK NESBIT: I would like to comment on another group of people who are forgotten. These are grandparents. The grandmother of whom it is said; "Oh don't tell her, you know it is going to be too hard on her," I found that this is another area where people have not been included in the process of dying. You know sometimes they are not ever told. They have been forgotten a great deal in our society.

DR. STACEY DAY: Thank you. Throughout every panel that we have had, including this one thus far, the importance of the family and loved ones and friends in comforting either the children or in comforting themselves, has been a primary discussion point. A person made an observation at the end of the last panel - I think she came to my office and proposed it to me. I am presenting that question to you because I think it is not only important from the point of view of the child, but also of adults. How would the panel deal with an orphan, that is a person who does not have the conventional loved ones about him. He does not have the friends that we have all been discussing in the entire three panels and although this is a pediatric panel and we are talking about children, I think at the back of my mind this also must surely occur in the elderly, in those tucked away in homes, who are in that sense orphaned, in the sense that they do not have friends or anybody to comfort them in the moment of death. It would appear to me that this is a problem. A problem for us all and it is a very human situation. How are you going to deal with it? I will start with John Brantner.

DR. JOHN BRANTNER: In the ideal society, there would be nothing like an orphan. There would be no such thing. There would be no person who through death of his parents is orphaned. We are trying to do that in our own society. We are succeeding a great deal better than we did 25 years ago. There should be nobody, who because of death or disappearance of a biological parent, is left without warm, supporting, teaching parental figures. This is a goal that we must all, of course, fight for. It brings up one thing I thought of earlier when we were talking about the death of a dog and the learning that might come from that. One cannot in one sense replace a loss through death. But in another sense we can and we do and we must. The whole process of grieving is to find the meaning of completing our lives again, in relationships, although one particular relationship has been destroyed. The working with what you describe, the social isolate, the person who is without the means of social support, without friends, without parent figures, without sibling figures and so on. In one sense this perhaps represents the kind of person who is least of all touched by death if he has already encapsulated himself through his own wishes or through society's imposing it on him So that if his life overlaps significantly with no other life, then the death of no other person can touch him.

DR. STACEY DAY: Thank you John. Ed, I want to pass this to you. I would imagine (I certainly have a personal view of a man of the cloth of any denomination as being a sort of parent figure) you must see a great deal of similar situations. Would you take this question.

FATHER ED MATHIE: In a sense I do see people frequently like this. Not just children, but old folks, and as you might know Stacey, in a car accident that happened not too long ago, people who were not from this area and had no one to be there when they were in the intensive care unit and things like that. I think a lot of the burden falls on the nurses and perhaps the doctors who are there, who are too busy really to listen to and care for or hear what they are asking, for in just a sense of someone to spend time with them - now they can't, so I would say who do they find who can fill up this time for these people? I find that when I personally get the real privilege or opportunity to be with persons like this it is great, fulfilling, and they are most grateful to be able to talk and say something to someone. So I would say the burden is on calling. I don't know who you call - seminaries, people, whoever, to say they are really not particular about *who* the person is but, they would like *someone* I think to talk with.

DR. STACEY DAY: Yes John.

DR. JOHN BRANTNER: There are, by the way, two volunteer groups from the Twin Cities that can be called upon. One out of Wesley Methodist Church and the other out of the Saint Paul Urban Parish. Two fairly large trained groups of volunteers whose job is, in the one case, restricted to calling on dying people who are alone and in the other case, Saint Paul Urban Parish, calling, visiting, making themselves friends with, inserting themselves in the lives of lonely and disadvantaged people - mostly sick people and very elderly.

DR. STACEY DAY: Yes, Florence Kahn.

NURSE FLORENCE KAHN: I just want to make one addition to the comment about how busy the nurses are.

DR. MARK NESBIT: You aren't asking for a raise now?

[Laughter]

NURSE FLORENCE KAHN: No not now. I guess the fact that nurses work around the clock and that they are kept busy is certainly true. Presently in some stations in this hospital, a new system of care delivery is used: *primary nursing*. A nurse is assigned to a patient when he is admitted and she is his primary nurse. She is not only responsible for making sure that there is a continuity of care for 24 hours, but by the process of time that she puts in from shift to shift, she does in fact become his friend and develop enough of trust relationship to give him something to hang on to. I wanted to briefly describe it here because I think it is relevant to this question. On Masonic I, where you have adult cancer patients and on the two pediatric stations with primary nursing, you will have a child or adult that dies before the relatives can get there. Being with the patient at that time is the main concern of the primary nurse.

DR. STACEY DAY: Thank you very much. I think that is very interesting and I think very important. Mulford Sibley have you anything to say.

PROFESSOR MULFORD SIBLEY: No.

DR. STACEY DAY: George Williams.

DR. GEORGE WILLIAMS: Yes I think there is another group of people that meets this hypothetical problem and that is the people working in the School of

Nursing and, of course, our friends working in Public Health Nursing. And many times these are the people who may well have the first contact with this hypothetical child that we are talking about and in my own experience they do an excellent job handling it either at their own level or making referral to an appropriate agency.

DR. STACEY DAY: Thank you very much.

DR. MARK NESBIT: I would like to comment on a *purposeful* orphan. It is something that I have experienced here in Minnesota. There seems to be a great number of parents in the Upper Midwest, who as far as children are concerned, have the attitude that when you bring a child to a hospital with an incurable disease, the physician is to take care of him entirely. (It's kind of like the farmer who says - if you have a question about farming, I'll take care of it; if it is a question about doctoring, you take care of it!) The parents kind of escape from the problem. They kind of leave. This is not like the East Coast where there are 150 relatives next to the bed fighting for space and asking every possible question. Here at the University I have seen a lot of children who are sent down here and the parents never come to see them. It is not because they do not care. If the child gets better, the child is included back into the family in a very organized manner. During the interim, the parents are not at the hospital. It is necessary and these children will search for support and will glomp onto someone in the hospital as a substitute parent figure. If the hospital personnel don't respond, and if you don't respond adequately, you have really lost the situation of helping this child. Many of the nurses react: "Oh this child is being left!" Now it isn't that the child has been purposefully left, because the hospital is responsible for taking care of him and are the ones responsible for not making this child an orphan. If you don't take this responsibility, I think you have really missed something.

DR. STACEY DAY: Thank you very much. Jasper Hopkins. *"Do children fear death? Or do they see it as part of living?"*

PROFESSOR JASPER HOPKINS: Well as we were suggesting earlier, their attitude is molded through their parents. It is not so much a question of whether their parents are religious or non-religious. If the parents treat death matter-of-factly, the child can come to view it that way too. As long as nothing disruptive occurs in the nucleus of the family. Let's put it this way; from his nature or from instinct, the child doesn't fear death. It is a learned thing and he picks it up from his environment.

DR. STACEY DAY: Mulford.

PROFESSOR MULFORD SIBLEY: Yes I would tend to agree with everything that has been said on this point, that the attitude to death is not, "instinctive" in any sense of the term, if that term has any meaning at all. But it is learned.

DR. STACEY DAY: John Brantner.

DR. JOHN BRANTNER: Yes. As with all of

our attitudes and expectations, beliefs and so on, our racial prejudices, our foods, dislikes, and preferences, our religious choices, all of these are instructed things and we acquire at least a groundwork for them by about the age of 4. So it comes directly from our parents. The matter of the instinctive thing. Not an instinctive fear of death, but there seems to be a kind of instinctive and perhaps a prehuman kind of reaction to some aspects of especially violent death. The insides of bodies, bodies which are incomplete, mutilated bodies, bodies without heads, bodies without arms, or bodies where the inner portions have become outer portions and perhaps the blood. These are universally feared.

DR. STACEY DAY: Thank you. George Willaims *"Is death reversible for the child? Will the dead one come back?"*

DR. GEORGE WILLIAMS: This is a very common thought that children have because it fits into their own defensive systems and it solves the problem for them. We see them acting this out in play all the time. It is a counterphobic phenomena to which I referred earlier. Frequently, when the child has lost a loved pet, and a pet is a person to a child, and the family has handled the funeral appropriately, the child now has gone through the ritual and now wants to get a shovel and dig him up. This is partly his denial and again it is the normal kind of thing. It is also a very healthy kind of thing. To say that he fears death - I don't know that he knows

the concept, so he may very well not fear death, but I think he may well be scared to death of dying.

DR. STACEY DAY: This is a very good point and a very good distinction. I would like to underline that point myself. Ed Mathie?

FATHER ED MATHIE: I don't know much about the situation. I have listened to some of the others give their answers.

DR. STACEY DAY: Mark Nesbit.

DR. MARK NESBIT: No, I don't think they fear death, they fear what we are going to do to them though. They fear the fact that I put them on cortisone and they become obese. They won't go to school and they will sit in their room instead. They will often tell me; "I would rather die than be on cortisone." They would rather die than have their hair fall out and *that is what many of these children fear*. The other thing they fear is the fact that they are not going to be able to discuss their anxieties with their parents - that the opportunity will never come. Especially with the teenager, parents feel that they haven't achieved anything. Parents give this idea; "Oh it is such a disappointment that this child is going to die because he can't become President of the United States!" Who would want to be President. Other concerns of parents are that their child hasn't gotten married. The teenager doesn't have those wishes, but the parents are disappointed that they haven't and they aren't able to discuss it. When the teenager finally realizes that he is dying, they are afraid of what is going to happen to the people closest to him and he would like to discuss with his parents that he has had a good life. I think at least in the teenager, the inability to communicate is what they fear most of all. The fact that they are not able to discuss with the people around them their past life and what they have accomplished.

NURSE FLORENCE KAHN: Can I add one comment to that? Let me just take it back one bit further in terms of the child really fearing procedures, because this is what the nurse deals with every day. A child, depending upon his individual strengths, will come in with just so much ability to cope. If you had to have bloods drawn in your arm two and three times a day, for six weeks in duration, you would begin to get a little drained by the end of that time.

[Laughter]

I didn't mean it.

PROFESSOR MULFORD SIBLEY: Oh you did too.

NURSE FLORENCE KAHN: Anyway I guess what bothers me most is that the nurse tries to prepare the child. She holds his hand and helps him hold onto his coping strengths, but with many fearful procedures coping begins to slip away. Take the little girl I am dealing with right now. I come in and I begin to look up at the IV flask and she begins to cry uncontrollably. This worries me. With long term leukemic children the nursing support through all of the daily blood drawing and IV medications is

crucial to how fearful the child becomes.

DR. STACEY DAY: Thank you very much. Let's pick out one we could all answer. *"How should hospital personnel react to a child's death?"* How would you have hospital personnel react to a child's death, Mulford Sibley?

PROFESSOR MULFORD SIBLEY: Well I think that question came up in general in the first panel. What should be the attitude of the janitor and other personnel and I would say precisely the same thing that I said then - the employee should, if possible, cultivate a genuine interest in what is going on about him. Our civilization is tending so often to be more and more impersonal that the more we can cultivate a kind of empathy, not only with the dying, but with the living, the better off the world will be.

[Applause]

DR. STACEY DAY: Thank you. George Williams, *"Do you see a difference between the child's death and the death of an adult patient in terms of how hospital personnel should react?"*

DR. GEORGE WILLIAMS: I think that the death of a child is much more difficult for hospital personnel to handle, because I think that it always seems so unfair when a child dies for whatever reason. When a child precedes its parents in death, this seems almost like an unnatural thing. I think very frequently people identify with this child through guilt, through empathy,

69

through love, whatever it might be and I think that this is a different ball game in a sense than the death of an adult. As far as treating the situations any differently, no I don't think so. I think they ought to be treated as has been pointed out.

DR. STACEY DAY: Ed Mathie. *"Should children be exposed to death? For example, should a child see a grandparent dying, do you think?"*

FATHER ED MATHIE: Well if they are in a hospital I guess they can't get in. But I think it is good and most books will say, that if they can, yes. I would just like to go back one if I could - just for a very short response. I think that the difference between an adult and a child, for the personnel, is that we have less to say to the parent. All we can really do is be there and show them how emotionally and how much that child really has meant to us. Because I think we are at a loss for words, at this time we might tend not to come or we don't know what to say, so we are more fearful than ever with an adult. That is more important.

DR. STACEY DAY: Fine. We have a few moments left and I am going to ask the panel a very difficult question. It would appear to me, in a generalized way, that there is a correlation obviously between death and living. I did a little exercise with John Johnson, who taught me physiology many years ago. I asked him what "life" was. I am going to ask each of you the same question and I am going to give you a couple of minutes to think about it before I put you on the

spot. I realize that this is impromptu. You did not know the question was coming, nor did you have time to go to the library to dig up an answer. I want each of you to tell me in a moment your definition of life, your personal definition of life, and then after that I am going to ask you to personalize your thinking - to tell me why you are living? Why each of you on this panel is alive? Your reason for living.

DR. MARK NESBIT: Do we get to ask you.

DR. STACEY DAY: You can indeed ask me but I have the privilege of cheating because I have thought about this over the last week. But to give you a few minutes to think it over while I sort of bring matters to a close - this is what John Johnson suggested as a definition of life. You will know that Jack is a physiologist and as you might expect, his reasoning is in scientific terms. Half of the panel are not physiologists and I therefore think the value of the exercise is to get a point of view that is not scientifically oriented and is not necessarily physiologically oriented. I will read you Jack's definition of what life is. He says:

"Life is a state of organization of matter. The atoms which are arranged in the patterns we call life are not unique but are found throughout the universe. As in a flame stability depends on a flow of matter through the pattern.

Life appears to be the most complicated state of organization - at least for a given volume of space - that we know. Separation of Universe into living and non living is simple at the extremes - e.g. an inert gas versus a human being, but when attempting to distinguish between the most complicated non living state and the simplest living entity (e.g. a virus), we have difficulty because our ability to classify degrees of complexity is not refined enough.

Death from this point of view then is an irreversible (at least of as now) perturbation in the pattern which precludes the activities associated with the state of organization called life."

Now Jack had the advantage of thinking over his reasoning - so you at least, so unfortunately caught, need at least a moment or two.

Thinking of all discussions raised in our three panel dialogues, one must of course never forget that we are most certainly not the first civilization to discuss attitudes towards death. The writings of Seneca, Socrates, Plato - indeed the ancients of *all* cultures wrote of death. Indeed I found the good advice of John Brantner that we should think daily on our own death, recited in the oldest Egyptian book of Moral Precepts extant . . . *"When the messenger of Death cometh to carry thee away, let him find thee prepared."*

That was written in 3500 B.C.! The essayist Montaigne was even more magnificently eloquent:

"I am at all times prepared as much as I am like to be . . . we should always, as far as in us lie, be booted and spurred and ready to set off."

I feel and have felt throughout all these panels, that if we are ready for death ourselves, we can more intelli-gently prepare others in the same attitude toward death.

On our panels, and I am not sure we haven't all run away from the fact, John Berryman was to have been a vital member. Many of us knew him, knew many of his moods. He was a literary historian and I know could have added much to our thinking. I thought about whether we should raise this question of him having been a prospective member of our panel in respect of his recent death. Each of you will have a viewpoint. I am not sure if Berryman has answered a question on death or raised a question on death. In my own thinking he seems to raise the problem of *getting beyond* death. John Berryman has got beyond death. Do we inevitably get beyond death? We see this attitude toward death commonly in writers and poets. You may recall Swinburne:

"Here now in his triumph, where all things falter,
Stretched out in the spoils that his own hand spread
As a God self slain on his own strange altar,
Death lies dead."

Or Shelley in Adonais:

"He lives, he wakes - 'tis death is dead not he."

Perhaps by getting beyond death we may live, avoid Camus' Sysyphus-like world where we all are continually pushing our troubles uphill only to have them tumble down again. As a physician, I share the same personal philosophy as appeared in the observations of B. J. Kennedy in our first symposium. This teaching, in my view, stands out importantly for the medical student. B. J. Kennedy in effect indicated that unless one is sensitive and sympathetic, if he be void of these qualities, he is *unprepared* to meet the dying patient.

In my own experience, when I was an intern and resident, I thought of a physician as sort of a pilot guiding the ship of life into its last dock. Certainly this is not an absolutely unique notion, for life has frequently been compared to a voyage or journey. Perhaps you will allow me the privilege of quoting from the last verse of one of my own poems entitled "The Last Dock" written from an experience as an intern following the death of a patient on the ward on which I was training:

"Life has unloaded its cargoes
Let me only ease the last moment in time
Let the brave flags fly on the rough slop swell
Let me only say from the foot of the bed
I am your pilot
Come to guide your ship home to its last dock."

This is how I personally see the role of the physician at the death bed. I do not easily see why a physician should feel that death signifies a failure - unless of course it *is* a failure of a human sort - a failure of judgement.

I think the celebrated father of surgery, Ambrose Paré, had a fine perspective of the physician's role. Every student here, I am certain, will remember his words on his being congratu-

lated on the recovery of a wounded soldier:

"Je le pansai, Dieu le guerit" (I treated him, God cured him)

When all has been done, the physician, I think, should anticipate and face his patient's death as Dr. B. J. Kennedy has said earlier. In so doing, I believe that there will be continued growth both for the physician *and* the patient, right up to the end.

And speaking of "end" reminds me that when I asked my secretary much earlier to go to the art design division of the printers and create an intelligent poster for the symposium, I was surprised when she finally turned up with the poster with which you are all familiar.

"What is that horseshoe thing" I asked her.
"Omega" she replied, *"the greek letter omega - the last letter of the alphabet!"*
"But what has that got to do with death?" I was puzzled.
"Well" she replied, *"the artist thought it was a good way of* ending *it all, saying that death is the end of it all!"*

Well *is* death "the end of it all?" Perhaps that is the reason I now ask our panel to give their definition of life, and their reason for living. Mulford Sibley will you begin?

PROFESSOR MULFORD SIBLEY: Well to answer the first question, it just depends upon whether you are thinking of biological life or whether you are thinking of psychological life. And whether the body and the soul are somehow so inseparably intertwined that the soul can

72

not survive in some sense beyond bodily death. I am impressed, for example, by the work of the late philosopher C. J. Ducasse, *The Belief In A Life After Death*, in which he deals with these problems. Biologically you can define life in terms of the regular functions of life, excretion, nutrition and so on. When they are gone, biological life is gone, but this says nothing necessarily about the persistence, for example, the conceivable persistance of the soul or the psyche in some form. Memory, imagination, thought and so on beyond the dissolution of the body. And science teaches nothing about that. I would like to insist on that point. There is considerable literature on modern psychical research that will deal with this problem of survival: Hornell Hart, among others, for example, in *The Enigma of Survival* and the *Ducasse Volume*. What is the purpose? - the second question. I guess I would go along with those who say that the purpose, so to speak, is the enlargement or the development of the consciousness and awareness of the soul. This is the purpose of life. I would also raise the question as to whether this purpose is carried out in one incarnation. Dr. Ian Stevenson, who is Professor of Neurology at the University of Virginia Medical School, is now making his main research interest the study of the possibility of reincarnation and he has written a very interesting book called *Twenty Cases Suggestive of Reincarnation*. I had to get in my plug for psychical research at this point.

DR. STACEY DAY: Thank you very much indeed. That is very interesting and stimulating. Jasper Hopkins?

PROFESSOR JASPER HOPKINS: Well the French existentialist philosopher, Jean-Paul Sartre, talks about man, human life, as a futile passion. He says that human life begins on the far side of despair. A man realizes that he has to create values and to develop, let's say, rationally, and morally, and perhaps even spiritually. It is an opportunity to ask oneself whether there is any ultimate purpose to his existence - and perhaps in asking this question to ward off, if one can, the feeling of absurdity that is lurking around every corner, behind every event, and within every potential encounter one has with death as he faces the future?

DR. STACEY DAY: Thank you very much. Florence Kahn?

NURSE FLORENCE KAHN: I haven't got any philosophers to quote. I guess my definition is a very simplistic one. I said that life is the flow and sum of experiences encountered by an organism through its growth, from beginning and including the end. Such a definition of life can relate to a very small organism or one as complex as ourselves. When I talk about the meaning of life to me - we spend our whole life working on that and I just wrote down some words that are meaningful to me and I guess you have your own words too. And one is *challenges,* in terms of life's challenges to me and what I set up for myself as goals. One is *involvement,* not only in terms of my personal relationships, but the work

I am in as a nurse and the involvement I have with the children I work with. *Joys and griefs,* are very important to me in my life. The griefs we experience give us a balance and make our joys much more meaningful to us. And, *fulfillment,* because I think that we all search for some kind of fulfillment within each other that we can share with other people.

DR. STACEY DAY: Thank you very much. George Williams?

DR. GEORGE WILLIAMS: I can only add to what has been said, that to me, life is also the sum total of our whole experience. Purpose for life, it seems to me, is a highly personal kind of question that we have been asking ourselves for a long time. My own is to hopefully understand myself to the best of my abilities and to develop my potential to the best of my abilities, to live up to the kind of things which I think are important, namely integrity, sensitivity, empathy, being able to help people, etc. I would like to live just as long as I can be of help to other people.

DR. STACEY DAY: Thank you very much. Ed?

FATHER ED MATHIE: I guess I would equate life very much with love in the sense that I see life as the opportunity to share and to support and also to be supported by others, and in that I think the purpose of my life comes. I follow the Christian message in the sense that I hope that I again am able to, as George mentioned, live as long as I am able to be of support to other people and to

share. Also, I think I might mean that I am sharing something of myself in them supporting me.

DR. STACEY DAY: Thank you Ed. Mark?

DR. MARK NESBIT: I think life is the ability to ask questions. You can ask the major question of what is death? When you know the answer, then you are not living any more. I think that the purpose of life is the capability to answer the questions asked.

DR. STACEY DAY: Thank you very much. John?

DR. JOHN BRANTNER: Life is the spectacular and glorious reversal of the material world's inevitable march toward entropy. And certainly (at the other end of this march through the panel) to put it in other words, it is at the human level, the growth in personhood. The growth from a bundle of noisy potential, into a fully developed person. This growth occurs only through relationships. It cannot occur in isolation and therefore, the reason, I or any of us live, really is in our own growth in person, the development of our soul, whatever language we use for this and this is done principly through relations. I was almost anticipated by Dr. Nesbit. I will simply remind you that thinking of these same questions, a very great teacher, Gertrude Stein, on her own death bed, as she lay there thinking about the same kind of things that we are thinking about, was heard by her friends to murmur; "What is the answer?" But perhaps at about that time her perspective changed and as she died she said; "What is the question?"

PROFESSOR MULFORD SIBLEY: Did she repeat it again and again?

DR. STACEY DAY: I think this has been an absolutely splendid panel. In answer to Dr. Mark Nesbit's request that I too be asked to give my own reason for living I am happy to try. I would say that I find my best reason for living in the immortality of the human spirit - the degree to which I may contribute to that determines the worthiness of my physical life. The mortality of my body is of little consequence. And now on behalf of the Department of Pathology and the Student Medical Council, I thank the members of this panel and every panel, for contributing to your questions and for helping us all develop our own mental attitudes and view on death and perspectives of death. Thank you all.

Death and
The Black

DR. STACEY DAY: Pastor Curtis A. Herron you are a black and I am a physician and we are sitting discussing together attitudes towards death, primarily of blacks, although we have agreed to try to relate as many of our observations as possible to people in general, both black and white, as they may be seen through the eyes of a black. Definitively let me ask you the first question. *"Do you consider yourself a good sounding board for the feelings of the black community - and would you say that you could offer as good an insight into the death attitude of blacks as say could be obtained from a similar discussion with a black M.D.?"*

PASTOR HERRON: I think so. And I think so because I am probably more in touch with the formation of attitudes about

life and death than an M.D. would be. I am called upon to attend deaths probably as often as one M.D. would. Moreover, because I have an entry into homes that a doctor does not have, I can go when I am not called because the people are my parishioners. I council them and I am often called to advise them on all the common interests of life, such as working on the job, marriage, sickness or death. These kind of things a doctor is not often called upon to attend, he does not get to know people in all these areas - or if so, not nearly as deeply as I come to know them.

DR. STACEY DAY: Then in a way, I could say that you reflect many aspects - social, psychological, cultural even political thinking that might be raised in the black community? You will have the potential for a great insight in your comments on the black community?

PASTOR HERRON: I think so.

DR. STACEY DAY: Do you think that in questions of death and attitudes towards death, a white physician is culturally able to satisfy the needs of the black patient who is dying?

PASTOR HERRON: I say that would depend upon his sensitivity towards black people and their attitudes toward death. If he is sensitive, his colour will have nothing to do whether or not he is capable. It is his sensitivity that is important. And I have found that generally white physicians are not very sympathetic in their treatment toward the black patient and especially in terminal cases.

DR. STACEY DAY: That is very important. I have travelled in many countries, including Africa, and I have always found a so called "cultural attitude" toward death. The American situation is somewhat confusing because we have, I guess, blacks and whites as distinct "cultures" yet *of* the same culture. For a doctor at least, I would hope, the primary concern would be the patient irrespective of his colour. But you have suggested to me the *necessity* for a white physician to be sympathetic to the black patient. Now I am going to ask you point blank: *"Do you feel that there is some sort of implicit distinction (not necessarily meant) in the attitudes of physicians toward a black patient as opposed to their attitudes toward white patients?"*

PASTOR HERRON: I have not been in the presence of white doctors treating white patients, so I can't comment on that, but I would certainly suppose they would need to be sympathetic toward *anyone* who is to die. What I am saying, and what I have said, is that generally speaking, I do find that white doctors are not as sympathetic. I am not talking about this in a purely humanistic way - I am talking about their lack of understanding. I don't think they understand the attitudes of black people - their fears, suspicions, their ideas about death, and therefore they are not as feeling in their ministering to the patient as they might be if they had such understanding.

DR. STACEY DAY: Do you think that the black person has a different attitude toward death, toward religion, to God, than the white person in America? Are the fears of the black different?

PASTOR HERRON: Yes. I think that what is different about black religion and white religion is *what is emphasized.* The conception of God is one thing to the older black person and another thing to the white person. One conceives of God according to the situation in which he is in and according to his needs for that God. Black people have been an oppressed people. They needed a God who was a great deliverer, a saviour, a great Messiah, a God to be worshipped, a God who would help - perhaps not so much a God to be worshipped as a God who would come and who would help in time of need.

DR. STACEY DAY: That seems to me important. Does that mean that the attitude toward death of blacks is different from that of whites?

PASTOR HERRON: Well working on your question I would say that black people have different ideas about God and these ideas would affect their attitudes towards death. Their attitudes about situations in which they live, also affect their ideas about death. If you have been living in a very bad situation, terrible physical situation, death is not as bad - not as terrible a thing to you, to that person, as it would be to a person who has had it very well in life.

DR. STACEY DAY: I am inferring from what you say, and I might be wrong and you will have to correct me, but I feel from what you say that death can be accepted more easily, possibly by a black person than by a white person. Is that so?

PASTOR HERRON: That does seem to be true but there are other variables, other things that enter into consideration. I do think, however, that the end result, *with all the variables*, is that black people have a very religious way of dying and they approach death with assurance. Older black do. Now this is not true of young blacks because young blacks are not coming out of the same situation. They have not been involved in the same kind of church or religious atmosphere as older blacks have evolved in. Older blacks that I am talking about are blacks over 30.

DR. STACEY DAY: Do blacks fear death?

PASTOR HERRON: Yes, there is a great fear of death in blacks, especially older blacks. There is also awe and reverence involved in this fear, and there is what the Christians call the blessed assurance that God is going to save them even in death. The reason that this would be different from whites is because black religion has been a religion of hope. It has been a crises religion, because a God was needed to bring people through their many crises that were continually appearing in their lives. Survival was a religious thing for black people and so God was constantly coming and saving.

DR. STACEY DAY: Does this thinking occur in the Spirituals - what I call the Spirituals?

PASTOR HERRON: Yes, it is seen in them. It is most exemplified in the negro Spirituals.

DR. STACEY DAY: Would a white psychologist have anything to offer a black?

PASTOR HERRON: If he can understand where the black is coming from, if he understands the religious emphasis of the black situation, but I imagine that if he is approaching the black purely from an academic point of view, then he could not.

DR. STACEY DAY: In as much as a white psychologist probably could not understand Hindu culture unless he had been in India and examined its background and worked with Hindus. Unless one is familiar with blacks, at first hand, living in America alone doesn't give any priority of understanding of the way blacks may approach life or death?

PASTOR HERRON: It gives him priority in the sense that he is on the scene and if he wants to be sensitive he can. He can see and he can observe, but he cannot know by academia, by being in an institution.

DR. STACEY DAY: That is important. *"What role does the black family play in the support of each other in the process of grief and mourning, following the death of a loved one?"*

PASTOR HERRON: The older blacks are very philosophical about death. While there is a great fear, it is not as great as white propagandists would have us believe. But we are trying to avoid the political field. There is a great deal of fear in death relatively but I don't know whether blacks fear death more than whites. I do know that blacks have a theological approach to death generally, and it enables them to accept death in a way. Sometimes their attitude is resignation, and even better than resignation, some find real hope in death because the world situation has been so bad for them. They may say; "Man I'm going to go to Heaven one day," and even though they don't want to stop living, they know that when they die there is going to be "a better world."

DR. STACEY DAY: The family therefore, in your thinking does support each other?

PASTOR HERRON: Yes, mourning is not the terrible thing in death. For the mourning ones' grief is a piercing and painful thing but not so terrible that they cannot handle it within a reasonable time.

DR. STACEY DAY: Therefore, it could be said in a general way that their mourning might be a *happy mourning?*

PASTOR HERRON: In times past it was. Even now as a minister familiar with funerals I attempt, and am often successful, at trying to develop the funeral into a kind of celebration. Especially when we feel that the person who has died has been a loyal and faithful servant of God. There is no need for sorrow, you see, and so we attempt to effect a victory celebration. We attempt to testify to our young people that here is one "who has made it." He has paid off. He has done well. And so this is a happy occasion and we try to even bring victory songs - Christian songs - into the funeral for the preface.

DR. STACEY DAY: Can I say I am reminded of Louis Armstrong's jazz immortal rendering - "When The Saints Go Marching In, I Want To Be There in That Company." It is almost a sort of victory celebration. As if death could almost be joyful, as if one were almost marching into heaven in a ceremony which is a happy occasion rather than a sad one. In many cultures we see this. In the Jewish testament one may read that "death is a wedding." For the arabs in erstwhile years, riding into death was a glorious and noble ride into the gates of paradise. From what you have said, I would conclude that you feel that in general blacks have a healthy attitude toward death?

PASTOR HERRON: That is a value statement. Whether it is healthy or not I don't know. I think blacks are people who will do anything that they can to survive.

DR. STACEY DAY: Then they are really like whites.

PASTOR HERRON: Yes, maybe even more so. Their history points out that blacks have a strong desire to survive and will go through hell to survive, so that death isn't something that one volunteers for, it is not something that one looks forward to.

DR. STACEY DAY: At a white's death, the family would appear to be important. I have a feeling, which may be incorrect and you must correct me, that culturally one of the effects of slavery was that it broke up black society in terms of family units. When the blacks were slaves for example, a father could be sold into bondage and separated from his wife and children. The whole system of slavery was inconsistent with developing family units. Certainly this was a century or so ago, but have social conditions so changed so as to permit "reconstitution" of the black family, socially and emotionally. Is my thesis right or wrong to begin with?

PASTOR HERRON: It is historically right but it is not altogether right. I think studies show that there is a closer family tie among blacks than among whites.

DR. STACEY DAY: Can you convince me?

PASTOR HERRON: Yes. Black children are not nearly as disrespectful to black parents as are white children to white parents. Black parents need their children more than white parents need their children - hence black parents hold onto their children longer than white parents hold onto their children. Black children need their parents more than white children. And so the family holds onto one another more. Maybe it is an economic thing, I don't know, but for some reason they hold onto each other longer and more tenaciously than do whites.

DR. STACEY DAY: Is that an objective assessment? Do you have support for that thinking?

PASTOR HERRON: Objectively, from the point of view of economics. Black parents need their children. When you need somebody you hold onto them. Black children need their parents.

DR. STACEY DAY: Let us consider the death of children. How would blacks relate to the death of a child?

PASTOR HERRON: I couldn't imagine blacks relating any differently than whites to the death of a child. It is a very painful and piercing experience to have to go through. I think the hardest thing for black people, the hardest deaths, the most piercing and painful depths that I have seen, experienced and administered, have been those in the case of children.

DR. STACEY DAY: How do black children react if they know they are dying?

PASTOR HERRON: I have not come up under the same kind of religious background of "When the Saints Came

Marching In" in *young people*. Young blacks have become more like whites, not very religious and not very theological in their approach. Therefore, when they face death, they do so with nonchalance or irreverence or they approach it with great fear and with no hope.

DR. STACEY DAY: No hope?

PASTOR HERRON: No hope because they have no God to guarantee or to give them assurance. God is not as real to them as he was real to their parents.

DR. STACEY DAY: Now one of the questions I asked Mulford Sibley was a philosophical question. There has been a tendency among Americans for blacks to group in center city communities and whites to reside in the "urban city". Social problems arise and new potentials present. As would be true for those born in an Irish slum or on the streets of Calcutta, children born in the ghetto obviously have a *greater potential* for disease and early death. Thus it might be said that center city people are faced with an earlier death or an earlier possibility of death. Is it true first in your thinking and secondly, if it be true, how would you face it?

PASTOR HERRON: It is true that they are faced with earlier death. They see more violence, they experience more crises than whites who are not in the center city. I don't think that they even think about it. It is a way of life and they are not aware that it is very different from the way anybody else lives. I have had

that experience. I was very poor but I never thought of myself as being poor, because I didn't know how rich everybody else was until television was invented. Then I discovered how poor I was, but I didn't know before so I could live with it. I think the rage that has happened in the last few years happened because television so enlarged poor people that they became aware of the fact that they were disenfranchised, deprived, and all of that. But so far as death is concerned, I don't think that people think about it. It is a kind of thing that they deal with when it comes to them and they don't anticipate it. I don't think that young people handle this too well. As for older people, I have administered to many people and watched them die and older people die bravely, courageously. They die with strong testimonies and they die with a kind of assurance and a certainty that God is going to deliver them. But young people, as a rule, do not have this kind of courage. They may die nonchalantly, they may give their lives. Young blacks in this day will give their lives only to prove that they are men.

DR. STACEY DAY: In what way?

PASTOR HERRON: It is difficult to go into this sort of political thing. When blacks finally came to realize how disenfranchised they were and how deprived they were, and how emasculated they had been by the dominant culture, then they immediately began to get themselves psychologically free of the dominance. They wanted to prove that they did not need the majority's approval in order for them to be men and so they ran out into the streets, they ran without weapons against police and against the national guard and against the power structure and were often cut down. They knew that they didn't have a chance and they did this because there was, in them, an important drive to prove that they are men. I think this is related to the fact that blacks were attempting to demonstrate to themselves and to the world, that they were men.

DR. STACEY DAY: But isn't this a so called "heroes' death." I would look upon this as sort of a black equivalent of the heroes' death. Isn't this also common to whites in a sense that they might not themselves see. Remember Tennyson's Charge of the Light Brigade.

"Their's not to reason why
Their's but to do and die."

PASTOR HERRON: It may be common to the white, but I am saying it is for a different reason and I think that it is important for physicians to know and be able to distinguish the reason. They may appear to be the same, a young black may be dying in the same way that a white is dying, but he is more than likely dying for a *different* reason.

DR. STACEY DAY: That is very good.

PASTOR HERRON: He may be dying in the same place but he may be dying for a different reason.

DR. STACEY DAY: I understand.

PASTOR HERRON: Psychologically, he is doing something to prove to himself this is what the culture has done to him, what the dominant culture has done to him. It has placed a burden on himself to make him strive excessively to be a man.

DR. STACEY DAY: Can you visualize a future situation coming, let's say, when life ends on a common plane for all men in the U.S.?

PASTOR HERRON: I want to say yes, I think so. But if I said that, then I would have to decide also that in time the church will become less powerful. The influence of the church will have become less powerful in the lives of black people than it is now and I think that is something that I don't like to think about. Yet I suppose it is true. Yes, I think so.

DR. STACEY DAY: Now from what you have said, and everything you have said seems reasonable, would it be reasonable to believe that because of the difficulties in the living of black people, the attitude to life they thus form would better fit a black M.D. to be more sympathetic or empathic when attending the death of a white patient, than has been the case you cited earlier of a white physician in attendance upon a black patient?

PASTOR HERRON: Generally a black person who has gone through medical school and has become a doctor, has developed attitudes that will not be very different from whites. Yet he has the connectional relationships to understand blacks, but having been in a white institution all his life, he has no problem in understanding whites. The truth is that blacks understand whites much better than whites understand blacks. This has been necessary for their survival. It was necessary for blacks to understand whites in order to survive. But it was not necessary for whites to understand blacks and so they did not have to, nor have they ever tried to. This is why a black physician could work well with whites, but a white physician may or may not be able to work well with blacks.

DR. STACEY DAY: I want to ask you whether a black physician educated in essentially a dominant white culture, on his return to a black community, practices through the thinking process of a white man. Is he sort of a black man with a white mind?

PASTOR HERRON: Certainly this depends upon the person, upon the sensitivity of the black person, the black M.D. Some of them try to forget whence they have come - many do forget. Others become very busy and rise above the struggle that blacks are very conscious of all the time. There is a struggle going on between blacks and whites or between blacks and the white power structure. We live with this awareness. Our children go to school with this awareness. Whites are not aware of it, but blacks are. The black M.D. who comes out of the white school rises above it and says; "I am so busy healing humanity that I

really don't have time to be part of that struggle." That is even provincial for he would say that is his way of rising above it.

DR. STACEY DAY: As a physician, can I ask whether you really feel that we can keep the political situation out of this? Death has social and psychological and other implications which derive from the society in which we live. This society is propelling us into political diversions. The point is, do you feel that it is inevitable that even in the situation of death and physicians, there must be political overlay?

PASTOR HERRON: I imagine that I have to believe that politics is a dominant factor in almost every aspect of life. Therefore, there would be at least some overlay, even in the way blacks approach death, as perhaps in the way whites approach death and the way a physician if he is white or if he is black, manages a black or white patient. I would say that politics has some overtones to this. You are speaking of politics in a very, very broad sense.

DR. STACEY DAY: Very Broad.

PASTOR HERRON: And in that sense, actually what you are speaking of is whether a physician is a humanist or whether he is not.

DR. STACEY DAY: I strongly believe in humanism. I would go further and say this, that don't you think if we educated ourselves as physicians and our medical students to face our patients as people, if we educated ourselves to be empathic and sympathetic and to face the problems of life and death as people, rather than white people or black people or indian people or japanese people, we would see the person who is dying as a person rather than as a black person or a white person. Do you think this possible or not possible?

PASTOR HERRON: I think generally that, as time goes on, an M.D. will be safe to approach a black person as if he were not white or black, just humanistic. Make a humanistic approach to him. But for a black person over 30 or 35 at least an M.D. would need to, should be aware of, that this man has an excessive fear of death and that he is theologically oriented and sees that there is hope in death and it would just be good for him to know that.

Could I suggest to you also that a very helpful approach for white M.D.'s when treating a dying black patient over 30, is to realize the fact that this person is more than likely to come out of a very religious background and has a theological approach to life and death. It would be well to attempt as soon as possible, if the person has one, to bring his minister into the picture and to talk with his minister about whether or not it would be well to tell the patient. A minister should have had such contact with the patient that the minister could say it would be all right to tell him or "no I don't think you should tell him." It is a religious thing you know.

DR. STACEY DAY: This reminds me of what Bob Fulton emphasized at one of the panel meetings. We, in the U.S., live in a two generational society. The older generation are moving farther and farther into old age and the younger generation is almost totally disassociated from the older generation.

PASTOR HERRON: I would say that.

DR. STACEY DAY: So in that one area, let's say there is an understanding between blacks and whites.

PASTOR HERRON: I agree with that. We have a common thing happening to us.

DR. STACEY DAY: That is a very important thing. Now we touched briefly on mourning and the mourning process. I have been told that blacks seldom bury their dead - that they in fact cremate the dead, whereas generally speaking whites bury their dead. Is this so?

PASTOR HERRON: I don't think that is true at all. In my life time, and I am forty years old, I don't know anyone who has been cremated.

DR. STACEY DAY: That is an important point.

PASTOR HERRON: I don't know of anyone who has been cremated. I have decided for myself that I would choose to be cremated, as an economic factor, because it would not cost my family as much as it would for a funeral. I think we spend too much money on funerals.

DR. STACEY DAY: What value do you see in a funeral?

PASTOR HERRON: I see a lot of value in a funeral. It is the time when we Christian people come together to celebrate and to demonstrate that here is life that has won, a life that has been well lived, and this is the way life could be lived and now we come together to remind each other of the promises of God, that, even if a man dies he can still live.

DR. STACEY DAY: In a psychological sense, grieving and mourning would have a role in your thinking?

PASTOR HERRON: We can soothe the mourning ones and we can give them assurance that this is not the worst thing in the world or the worst thing that could have happened in this life.

DR. STACEY DAY: Would you tell a black patient that he is going to die?

PASTOR HERRON: It would depend upon the patient. I would need to know how he approaches life. What his life is like. I feel more like talking with an older person about death than I would with a young person.

DR. STACEY DAY: Would you tell a black child that he is going to die?

PASTOR HERRON: It would depend upon his orientation to his religious back-ground. If he had the tools of religion to emphasize that there is a great hope for him in death, then I could talk with him about it. I could talk with him about the symbols of another life like angels and heaven and a good God, a loving father, and all the good things that there could be for him.

DR. STACEY DAY: Are black children in the habit of having pets?

PASTOR HERRON: Yes.

DR. STACEY DAY: As much, do you think, as white children?

PASTOR HERRON: No, but they have pets.

DR. STACEY DAY: If a pet dies, do you think that would help a black child face the reality of death?

PASTOR HERRON: I have seen black children have funerals for their pets.

DR. STACEY DAY: What sort of funeral? Could you describe one?

PASTOR HERRON: Well they were pained. It was really that they were emulating an adult funeral, I suppose. They were pained. But it was a sort of a mock funeral. It wasn't really something that they were deeply involved with. And then I have seen them when the whole family was involved in the funeral for the pet. You know it was a mock, it was something that was done as an informal thing, that was done in a back yard or on a hill someplace you know . . . .

DR. STACEY DAY: Would you say that is good?

PASTOR HERRON: It might be. It might be helpful.

DR. STACEY DAY: It was told in the panel, for example, that children play Cowboys and Indians and one will bang-bang the Indian dead. Then the Indian falls down and he gets up again immediately. Would you also find a parallel in black society. Do black children play cowboys and Indians and have the same fantasy images?

PASTOR HERRON: When I was a child I

did, but then that was a long time ago. They probably play Black Panthers versus the power structure now. I don't know what games they now play.

DR. STACEY DAY: That is interesting. Do black children see Santa Claus as black or white?

PASTOR HERRON: Since the black awareness has really come into being, a child would paint the face of Santa Claus black and with white hair.

DR. STACEY DAY: Santa Claus is a very old man!

PASTOR HERRON: Yes he is very old. They will paint the face of Jesus black also.

DR. STACEY DAY: With respect to older black people, are they shocked about death being sudden or violent?

PASTOR HERRON: I think it depends on how close they are to the person who dies. I think the difference is that there is a kind of resilience in the older Christian that is not found in the young person. For example, you tell a black patient that he has cancer and it would knock him off his pants if he is a Christian. He just goes all to pieces for a couple of days or a couple of weeks, maybe a month or two.

DR. STACEY DAY: The white patient also.

PASTOR HERRON: Yes, but a difference. What I am saying is a person with a religious background will bounce back. He has the resilience to bounce back. After he has gotten over the shock, he knows then his faith sort of takes over

as if it were a subconscious thing, just pervading his mind. It takes over and then hope begins to come into him and he remembers the promises that are real to him that *death is not all.*

DR. STACEY DAY: Then the physician could use this to work with the patient?

NASREEN DAY: There seems to be a difference between violent death and death, say of cancer.

PASTOR HERRON: It is hurting, it is painful, and it is shocking, but there is hope for the religious person. It is not there for the non-religious person.

NASREEN DAY: The grieving and mourning say when somebody who had cancer or a terminal patient finally dies, is there a sense of relief? When finally the suffering has ended. But the person who has had a violent death, how do they approach that? That's not the same . . . .

PASTOR HERRON: There is not the same relief.

NASREEN DAY: I am told even for an older person who died violently on the street, it is no longer being joyful the way you were saying before?

PASTOR HERRON: Celebration! It would be more difficult to pull off the celebration thing for a sudden death.

NASREEN DAY: It is, how shall I say it, not in your hands! God called the person who had cancer and he died - there is nothing any human individual could have done. But on the other hand, were it a violent death, at the hands of another human being, it could have been prevented. It could have been a tragedy that should not have happened. Would that effect be part of what affects the mourning?

PASTOR HERRON: Yes.

DR. STACEY DAY: Let us deal with euthanasia. What, in your opinion, is the attitude of the black community toward euthanasia. Is there a possibility at this time of blacks voluntarily asking for or choosing the moment of death?

PASTOR HERRON: No, no! Blacks are extremely guarded about life. They will do anything to live and they never want to die nor do they want to see their loved ones die. You must be aware that blacks, of all races, have the lowest incidence of suicide.

DR. STACEY DAY: No, I didn't realize that.

PASTOR HERRON: Life is an extremely precious thing, in spite of the fact that it is also a hurting thing.

DR. STACEY DAY: That might be corroborated by the painful nature of life in underprivileged or underdeveloped nations - suicide is uncommon in some Asiatics - India for example. Your feeling is that, at this time, euthanasia doesn't enter into black thinking - at this time?

PASTOR HERRON: It enters into the person who is dying. The person who is suffering would like to die, but he would probably not agree to death. It enters into the minds of the relatives who are attending but they would, more than likely, if they are older people, not

agree to it. If they were younger people, they might agree to it.

DR. STACEY DAY: Can you consider voluntary euthanasia - a patient asking voluntarily that his life be terminated?

PASTOR HERRON: Not among older blacks. Among younger blacks, yes. I would say yes.

DR. STACEY DAY: Bob Fulton said in terms of this two generational society that this is "the decade of death." Euthanasia is coming in the next 10 years and that soon, as in the last American war, the young generation will put a gold star in their window saying "we gave" - meaning that they gave their parents, their grandparents and everybody else. The implication is that they sent their parents away to die. This younger generation of whites would appear to isolate their elderly in nursing homes so that the old white is going away to die in relative isolation and not in the family setting. They may die sometimes slowly and sometimes neglected in a broader sense. Would you think this is true of the black community?

PASTOR HERRON: It is not true. Blacks hold on to their older people. It may not be a healthy thing that they do but they still hold on to their older people. They can't give them up in the same way, with the same ease, it appears to me.

DR. STACEY DAY: I would interpret this, then, that probably few elderly blacks are sent away to nursing homes to die.

One might find a greater number of older blacks still within the family setting?

PASTOR HERRON: Yes.

DR. STACEY DAY: And therefore there is a great difference here socially between the black community and the white community. In terms of death?

PASTOR HERRON: Yes, I would say that. But I would say that the trend will be toward becoming very much like whites and probably in 20 years, there will not be much difference in attitude.

DR. STACEY DAY: This suggests to me that it is an economic factor.

PASTOR HERRON: It may be.

DR. STACEY DAY: When the economic threshold of the black rises, you might adopt those attitudes which we identify with the white people.

PASTOR HERRON: Yes, unless the black movement to retain what has been a black thing, becomes continuous with great strength and black people begin to cherish and hold on to their traditions. If they do, then they may stem the tide of assimilating or becoming like the whites. And there *is* this possibility.

DR. STACEY DAY: Another problem. Another statement has been raised that death and sex are similar in this society in that they are both taboo. One doesn't want to talk about them and this is one of the reasons why we had this symposium - to get people to talk about death and face death. Is death taboo in that sense among the black?

PASTOR HERRON: You mean that they don't want to talk about it?

DR. STACEY DAY: Yes.

PASTOR HERRON: I will probably preach three sermons a year about death. But then I seize upon every occasion at a funeral to talk about death also. It isn't the most talked about thing, but it is talked about and older people give a lot of thought and talk about death. I don't know about young people, I just don't think they think about it. They may talk about it, but they don't do a lot of thinking about death.

DR. STACEY DAY: Would I be right in saying that throughout our conversation I feel very strongly that you, like whites, have drawn a great sort of differentiation between the two generations. Between the old generation and the new generation that you have suggested to me has revelations of the sort of continuity of the family as a unit in the blacks that it has lost in the whites. That would be one of the differences we discussed. But in general, blacks and whites see this great divide between the older generation and the so called new generation. It would appear, in a general way, that the new generation has more problems to face, in both life and death, than the older generation appears to have. Do you have any way of dealing with that?

PASTOR HERRON: Well, I try to have our church act as a counter culture. I try to emphasize the traditions of blacks that were good and to encourage the young people not to be caught up in the culture of the majority, but to reflect deeply upon what was good about the blacks and hold on to it.

DR. STACEY DAY: I am very much worried in a very personal sense by this gulf, this sort of divisions of communities. I understand historically, why the black people must seek identity, I do understand that. I understand, I think, the purposes surrounding the changes you are undergoing right now and I think these are important in raising what you call (I don't like the phrase) the dignity of blacks. I understand that. But it seems to me that black studies and all these expressions of blackness we see about us, are wrong. This is how it seems to me personally and I would have to say to be honest, that I don't like them either from the white side or from the black side. It seems to me that if I could have a divine right, the goal would be to bring about social changes that are valid for *all*. This is, after all, the United States of America, presumably one country. There obviously are differences of degree, but still, shouldn't the total goal be a oneness rather than such as black movements. I don't mean to be rude, but if I were to say that black studies are all nonsense, that we have to change the social faces of our communities, not our races, but change the society in which we live to get the best results, would you respond to me angrily or would you feel that I am wrong or would you feel that actually through the black movement, perhaps you can attain the goals I have described?

PASTOR HERRON: The goal for thinking blacks is the same as you have described, which is one humanism, a one humanity. And so blackness as a movement is not an end, it is not the goal, it is a means to the end. It is important for black people to affirm themselves as human beings, before they can become a part of the main stream of humanity and blacks must, in order to affirm their humanity, compensate for what has been taken away from them. Their humanity has been taken away from them. So they must first love themselves and in order to love yourself the slogan "black is beautiful", and all of these things, these slogans, were designed to overcompensate, to bring the child from being nothing to being, to make him feel superior to the whites. But in the long run, common sense will bring him back to the medium where he will discover that you are not really better than the whites, but as good as the whites. But you have to overcompensate, to reach down to bring him up, you see. So this is an intermediate strategy, one used to reach the goal which is one humanism. We can not begin to deal with white culture until we can believe in ourselves and love ourselves. There is self hatred among blacks and it was taught us by whites because we saw ourselves through white eyes. We only thought of ourselves as being whatever they thought we were. We thought of beauty as being based upon what whites thought was beautiful and we thought of goodness and most values as being only those values of whites and this was a very damaging thing for black people. An outsider would have much difficulty in understanding that until it was explained to him. So I can understand why you think like you think and it is natural for you to see that since the goal is oneness, that therefore, we must not talk about being different. But if you could understand that we are different, maybe we are not inherently different (perhaps there are even inherent differences) as you know physically there are some differences between black people and white people. We are different because culture has made us different. We are different for the other racial, ethnic or inherent reasons that we are different and there is no need for us to go around talking about how we are no different, when we are different. It is a truth. But we are not inferior and we have to make ourselves know that and it is going to take time for black people to finally understand they are not inferior.

DR. STACEY DAY: So this is sort of a growth process.

PASTOR HERRON: Yes, it is an intermediate strategy.

DR. STACEY DAY: Therefore, I as a non-black, have to be aware of this growth process as much as a black and therefore, I can only understand in terms of reference which you put for me. After you having told me your explanation, I have to mend my original question. Otherwise I don't grow myself and therefore there is an understanding required of me to see your point of view,

but, together, people can move in this way to understand that it would be a growth process. Now before I close, could I ask you one more question - as I asked each member of the panel? That would be to ask you your definition of life, and although it is personalized, your reason for living.

PASTOR HERRON: A definition of life? Well, for me there is existence and there is life, and I understand life to be a great stream that is going someplace, that has a destiny. It stands for something, that means something, and it is going ultimately to God. Moving toward God. Life stands for something and its meaning comes from God, you see. And its purpose? The purpose of life is to serve this God that we understand is at the end of life.

DR. STACEY DAY: Thank you so much. Is there anything you might like to add to our discussion - any thought you would add?

PASTOR HERRON: I am very much concerned how whites handle the subject of death. I would hope that they could become a lot more humanistic than they are. I really don't think that they are very humanistic.

DR. STACEY DAY: Towards blacks?

PASTOR HERRON: White physicians towards black patients.

DR. STACEY DAY: Do you think the white physicians attitude toward the white patient is different from the white physicians attitude toward the black patient?

PASTOR HERRON: It is my experience. I would have to believe that white people treat whites differently than they treat blacks.

DR. STACEY DAY: Pastor Herron may I quote you on our discussion?

PASTOR HERRON: You are free to quote me.

DR. STACEY DAY: Thank you very much.

A CLOSING NOTE

It is clear that in the limited time at our command, only a few of the many questions posed by the student body could be answered. The phenomena of death, like the phenomena of life, still remain.. very much uncircumscribed. For the medical student particularly, a sensitive study of death must pass far beyond the physiologic and pathologic laboratory door. History, mythology, psychology, theology are all, as our panels have so eloquently explored, within the compass of death education and research. Carrington has said that as long as science deals with *phenomena*, only the matter of death is likely to remain unsolved. Man must comprehend the *innermost* nature of things, including himself, to arrive at an ultimate view of his own place in Nature and in the universe.

Clearly innumerable questions remained to be asked and to be answered. Problems of aging*, problems surrounding death such as sleep, trance, catalepsy and suspended animation, and the so called "signs of death", all of which have from time immemorial, been matters of research and speculation for both physicians and philosophers. Even two decades ago *the moment of death* was but an academic concern. Today in the world of transplantation, the moment of death has been a *cause célèbre*, a veritable ground of disputation for physicians, surgeons, jurists, theologians and philosophers alike!!! It is a commendable thing that a physician or medical student of today can walk the wards ignorant of death, the *odor mortis*, avant courier herald of death of his professional brethren of a century ago, yet the banishing of this familiar clinical sense "of the existence of death during life" should not encourage neglect of a sensitive appreciation and awareness and ability to cope with problems of death when ultimately they do come. The quality of life has improved over the last years - so also should there be an improvement in the quality of the attitudes toward death, both in the professional health care services and in society universally. Towards this goal we hope our present panels and studies have contributed.

... Stacey B. Day

---

*Which Metchnikoff called "an infectious chronic disease" . . . "manifested by a degeneration, or an enfeebling of the noble elements, and by the excessive activity of the macrophags."